A SELF-DEVELOPMENT PROGRAMME

Effective leadership

Acknowledgements

The following individuals or organizations have kindly
contributed to approaches in this book: Dr Paul Dobson,
City University Business School; Col Ian Rodley, late 1st
Royal Tank Regiment; Royal Military Academy
Sandhurst; Peter Robinson.

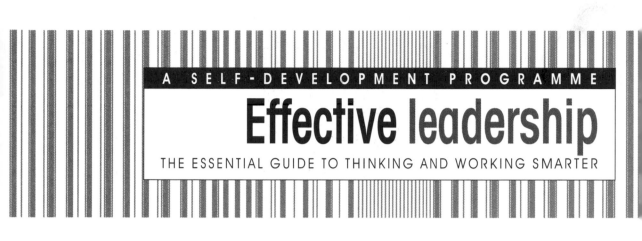

A SELF-DEVELOPMENT PROGRAMME

Effective leadership

THE ESSENTIAL GUIDE TO THINKING AND WORKING SMARTER

Chris Roebuck

MARSHALL PUBLISHING • LONDON

A Marshall Edition
Conceived, edited and
designed by
Marshall Editions Ltd
The Orangery
161 New Bond Street
London W1Y 9PA

First published in the UK
in 1999 by
Marshall Publishing Ltd

Copyright © 1999
Marshall Editions
Developments Ltd

ISBN 1-84028-200-2

Cover photography
The Stock Market

Series Consultant Editor
Chris Roebuck
Project Editor
Conor Kilgallon
Design
Joanna Stawarz
Art Director
Sean Keogh
Managing Art Editor
Patrick Carpenter
Managing Editor
Clare Currie
Editorial Assistant
Sophie Sandy
Editorial Coordinator
Becca Clunes
Production
Nikki Ingram
Cover Design
Poppy Jenkins

Originated in Italy by
Articolor
Printed and bound in
Portugal by Printer
Portuguesa

Video Arts quotes on pages 24, 35, 44, 49 and 60
extracted from the training film "Where There's a Will..."

299636

Contents

1

Introduction
Leadership and management
What do good leaders do?

Benefits of good leadership
Costs of bad leadership

Introduction

The ability to lead is the one crucial skill that those who have to get the best out of a team, an organization or a nation, must have. Leadership is seen as something that sets an individual apart from the rest. The aura that surrounds the skill elevates it to a mystical quality, one that many believe you can only be born with. However, this is not true. This book will show you how leadership works and how you can improve your current skills.

Myths and preconceptions

People assume that unless you're a chief executive, a general or a president, you're not really a leader. Again, this is not the case. If you run a team of any sort, even of only one other person, you are a leader. Those who lead large groups of people just need better skills than most – the more people you lead, the harder it is.

Although surrounded by a mystique not associated with other skills, leadership is really a simple idea: it is the ability to get the best out of your team in any given situation.

If you can show that you can do this, everyone will benefit. Your team's performance will improve, individuals within the team will develop, your company will grow and you yourself may be promoted.

Is there a difference between leadership and management? Some say that leadership is part of being an effective manager and others that management is part of being an effective leader. To help you think about the distinction, look at management as dealing with the preparation, planning and decision-making aspects of a project, and leadership as getting the team to complete the project – the communication, motivation, delegation and supervision.

You could say that managament turns ideas into plans and leadership turns plans into successful action. For any job to be completed successfully, you need skills in both areas.

What do good leaders do?

It will help you to start to understand leadership if you think about a boss you really respected and trusted. Think about what he or she did that made them special, the things that other bosses did not do. If you write down their key actions, this will give you an idea of the way good leaders work and also show you what you should be trying to do yourself.

To look at this from another perspective, write down the things you would like to see your team leader doing. Your ideal leader will probably:

- Keep you informed on what's going on
- Respect your professional skills
- Help you develop your skills and further your career
- Show genuine interest in you as a person
- Give you responsibility through clear, achievable objectives
- Tell you how you're doing in a constructive way
- Give you praise when due
- Be prepared to help out when things get busy
- Understand what motivates you and use this to help you work better
- Admit to mistakes and be prepared to say sorry
- Support you and back you up.

The more people you have to lead, the better your skills have to be to do all these things and get the job done. But as you build in experience this ability will develop naturally, and if you follow the list above, you can't go far wrong.

How can I do these things?

But how can you make sure you are doing these things all the time? Although the list seems fairly simple, once you add in the pressures at work, following it becomes more difficult. To help you overcome this problem, there are some simple, practical formats that can help you in this book.

Much has been written on leadership from historical, technical, psychological and theoretical points of view, but few books set out to help and encourage individuals to develop the skills of leadership.

The objective of this book is to help you to improve these skills. It is not an examination of the different theories of leadership or a discussion of the differences between management and leadership. Here we will concentrate on improving your skills, by implementing simple, practical, ideas, combined with your own past experience and the experience you will gain by trying new approaches.

Varying your style

As leadership is defined as getting the best out of the team in any given situation, you need to be able to vary how you lead to match different situations. You might say that work doesn't change much, but have you ever had two jobs that were really identical? Take a moment to list three jobs you do regularly. Were they really identical, or was some factor different? Jot down which factors were different.

It would be very surprising if all three jobs had not varied from week to

Introduction

week in some way. If this happens with everyday tasks, think of the different approaches unexpected projects will demand.

Because the objective of leadership is to get a job done, the skills you need are "task related". Initially, you need to plan the task, possibly involving the team. Therefore, there are some "self-leadership skills" to consider, particularly time management, prioritizing and planning. These will ensure that you can organize the team to complete the task, on time, by doing the most important jobs first.

Foundation skills

The first lesson of leadership consists of learning the "foundation skills" of delegation (getting the best people to do the right jobs), communication (making sure everyone knows what to do) and motivation (making sure everyone wants to get the job done). These three areas interlink and once they are in place you can move onto the "advanced skills" – creating vision, values and team spirit.

Underpinning it all are the critical leader behaviours, which enable you to build credibility and gain the respect and trust that will enable you to obtain the extra performance from your team you would not otherwise get. These

relate to the way you treat people and are important not only at work, but in life in general.

Without these principles, no matter how good you are at communicating, delegating or motivating, your team will not trust or respect you, and as a result, your ability to be an effective leader will be restricted.

The leader and the team have a special relationship perhaps not present between team and manager. Leadership involves turning a group of individuals into a team. How would you say you are doing at the moment? One key question you can ask yourself is, "would I follow myself?" Do you think you encourage mutual respect and trust from your team?

If you assembled your team and asked them if they thought you were a good team leader what would they say? Would you even have the courage to ask? Would they be frightened of giving you an honest answer? Do you even have any idea what they would say?

Just take a few minutes to honestly think about what would happen. You can then judge yourself against the 'good leader' activities you listed earlier. Even if you think you know what your team thinks of the way you lead, there are probably things you are unaware of.

Leadership today

The way we now work, and how people expect to be treated, means that leaders have to build relationships, rather than coerce, to be effective. Times have changed considerably in the past two decades, and power and position are no longer enough; you cannot demand respect, you have to earn it. Leadership is, more than ever, a two way process – in the end, without willing followers, you cannot lead.

The benefits of good leadership are:

- The team works as a team not just as a group of individuals. It works to a common objective
- The team is able to understand its objectives and how these fit in with overall organizational objectives
- Team members support each other
- The team is prepared to put in extra effort when required
- The team aims for excellence, not just "doing the job"
- Everyone knows what the team has to do, and their role
- The team are motivated to do the job as effectively as possible
- The specific tasks within the overall job are allocated to those best able to do them.

The costs of bad leadership are:

- The group are unclear on what they have to do. Time and resources may be wasted and the job may not be done properly
- The group is not motivated. They take longer than they should to do the task, or may not even complete it.
- The individuals are not working as a team, and will not perform as well as a team would
- The group will probably only do enough to get the job done and not be able to sustain a workload under pressure
- The group members will leave more often, as they will not want to stay in such an environment
- Individuals will not develop their skills and thus the group will be unable to deal with new situations.

2

Self-assessment Questionnaire

Good and bad leadership

Key components

How good am I now?

Before you can start to develop your skills, it is important to know how good you are at the moment. You will not then waste time trying to improve in areas where you are already doing well, so you can focus on areas which need the most improvement. You have already written a few notes on parts of your job that require leadership in the exercise in the previous chapter.

This chapter is designed to build on that first step by taking you through a general self-assessment process. By the end of it, you will be able to identify your strengths and weaknesses and be able to plan your own skills improvement programme.

Good and bad leadership

To start off, you first need to assess whether you lead effectively at work. You may find it useful initally to think about how leadership has affected your life over the years. Firstly, think about bad leadership: write down five incidents of bad leadership that you have experienced, including what went wrong, and the consequences.

To think about good leadership, go back to the list on page 9 on what people want from their leaders and consider how you perform in each one. Just put a rating of 1 to 10 beside each. For example, if you "give praise when due" on only half the occasions you should, put 5, if you nearly always "give responsibility using clear achievable objectives", put 9. Be honest with yourself – if you aren't, then you won't gain any benefit from the exercise.

Key components

Let's now look at the different key components of leadership we use most often. To do this, answer the questions in the boxes on the next three pages. Each assessment will focus on one area in particular, and this will allow you to fine-tune the development assessment you will do later in the book by seeing where you have strengths and weaknesses.

At the end of each section, you can analyse your answers. Make sure you give honest answers: you must say what you do in practice, not what you know you should be doing!

Questionnaire

Answer the following questions and tick the answer – "usually", "sometimes" or "seldom" – which best describes what you do, how you behave or what usually happens.

Meeting organizational needs	Usually	Sometimes	Seldom
1. I check if the team is really fulfilling the needs of our customers or clients			
2. Team members are aware of how their jobs fit in with organizational objectives			
3. I make sure that I am aware of organizational vision and objectives			
4. We create a team vision and objectives from the organizational ones			
5. I let the team contribute to achieving our vision and objectives			

Time management and prioritization	Usually	Sometimes	Seldom
1. I plan my time in advance so I know what I should be doing and when			
2. I allocate a priority to different tasks			
3. I have a daily 'to do' list			
4. I do the jobs others cannot do and delegate to them those they can			
5. I give maximum priority to jobs that help achieve our team objectives			

Planning and objectives	Usually	Sometimes	Seldom
1. When the team has been given a task I take time to plan how we will complete it			
2. I set myself clear objectives (specific, measurable, realistic and timed) for each task			
3. When a task comes up I weigh up different options to do it not just jump to a conclusion			
4. I make sure that I have a "back up" plan in case there are problems			
5. I work out how long a job will take before accepting it			

Delegation	Usually	Sometimes	Seldom
1. I check that people have time to take on more work before delegating to them			
2. I give people as much responsibility as possible when delegating to them			
3. I use delegation to help develop the skills of team members			
4. I regularly assess if I could delegate more jobs as the team's skills improve			
5. I agree the level of freedom I give individuals with them before they start the job			

Questionnaire

Briefing people	Usually	Sometimes	Seldom
1. When briefing I make the objectives clear, so everyone knows exactly what is required of them			
2. At the end of a briefing I ask for questions to make sure everyone is happy			
3. During a briefing I tell people the background to what I am going to say			
4. I give individuals a clear reporting structure so they know when to come back to me			
5. When briefing I explain how our work fits into the bigger picture			

Communication: giving feedback on performance	Usually	Sometimes	Seldom
1. I give feedback to individuals on their performance on a day-to-day basis			
2. When discussing performance problems I use them as a reason for development			
3. Before giving feedback I make sure that the other person is listening and we are not going to be disturbed or distracted			
4. I allow the others person to give their views before I give mine			
5. I end the feedback on a positive note even if it has been negative feedback			

Communication: getting feedback and listening	Usually	Sometimes	Seldom
1. Team members come to me with ideas to improve team or individual performance			
2. I ask my team how I could help them work more effectively			
3. When talking to team members I spend as much time listening as I do talking			
4. I hold regular team meetings to brief the team and get their views			
5. I ask the team for feedback on my performance			

Motivation	Usually	Sometimes	Seldom
1. I use different approaches to motivate different team members			
2. When deserved I give praise to team members for a job well done			
3. If possible I offer individuals a challenge and opportunity to develop via their work			
4. I make sure I speak to every team member for a few minutes every day			
5. I always think about how best to allocate jobs to maximize individual's motivation within the team			

Developing the team	Usually	Sometimes	Seldom
1. I am aware of the skills team members have and their development needs			
2. I match team development needs to the skills needs of the team required by team and organizational objectives			
3. Each team members has a development plan which is agreed with me			
4. I coach individuals to improve their skills and encourage other experienced team members to do so			
5. I have my own skills development plan which I regularly update			

Creating vision and team spirit	Usually	Sometimes	Seldom
1. I let the team know how they contribute to the "bigger picture"			
2. We have special functions or activities to build team spirit			
3. We have a team mission which sets out how we will achieve our vision			
4. We discuss and agree our team mission and vision			
5. Team members are encouraged to support and develop each other			

SCORING

In each area, score 3 points for "usually", 2 for "sometimes", and 1 for "seldom". Add up your total. If you score:

13-15: You are doing well at the moment, but with a little effort you could be very good.

10-12: Your team are probably getting the job done but with some work you could be leading them better and they could then perform better.

5-10: This area is not one of your strengths but you can improve your skills with a little thought and practice.

Under 5: This is an area in which you need to urgently develop your skills. It is probable that this area may be restricting both your, and the team's, performance in other areas as well. Don't worry – with effort and planning you will improve.

So what now?

This will have given you an idea of how you are doing at the moment. If you want really accurate answers, why not be brave and ask your team how you perform in each section? Having got a feel for where your skill levels are at the moment, the next chapter will help you gain a better understanding of leadership and its component parts.

3

Understanding leadership
Critical principles
Foundation skills

Advanced skills

Giving feedback

Coaching

Understanding leadership

"It is a terrible thing to look over your shoulder when you are trying to lead – and find no one there." Franklin Delano Roosevelt, former US President

In this chapter we will look at how leadership works, both in general and then specific terms. This will help you to understand leadership and adopt the best practices for future uses.

As we saw in chapter one, you may have been led to believe that leadership is a skill that cannot be learnt. Such myths usually come from those who don't really understand leadership.

Remember that leadership skills do not automatically improve as you become more senior. So first, let's deal with these myths:

- *"Leaders are born, not made."* No. leadership skills, like any other skills, can be developed with knowledge and practice.
- *"A leader must have certain, defined, qualities."* No. No list of qualities has ever been formulated that can apply to all great leaders. The important factor is the behaviour you demonstrate, not the qualities you have. Some behaviour may increase your chances of becoming an effective leader, as we will see later.
- *"Leaders in one situation must be leaders in others."* No, a person becomes a leader because they are the best choice to lead the team for a specific task; they may not be the best leader for a different task.
- *"Leadership can only be developed by experience."* No, development of any skill is a combination of passed-on knowledge combined with practice to build experience. Otherwise everyone would rely on trial and error alone.
- *"Leadership is not a popularity contest."* No, it is not, but if you are an effective leader your team will like you because you can motivate and develop them.

A balance

In general terms, ask yourself, "why and how does my team manage to do the job and not just fall apart?"

The answer is because you are holding it together with your leadership skills. You can think of leadership as a balance. One side is the effort that you are putting in to make the team effective, (team spirit, loyalty and co-operation) and on the other side are all those things that will make it want to give up (workload, stress, time pressure, danger).

As the team builds, you have to add extra effort to keep it going by motivating and supporting them more. In all situations your team faces, you must input sufficient positive energy through leadership to counteract the negative forces that might cause the team to fail.

Leadership equation

The leadership process

What is the process by which you lead your team through the tasks they have to do? Most tasks are started by either a direction from senior management or an event that needs a response. Ask yourself, "what do I need to achieve?"

Your next stage – consultation – is to make sure you have all the information you need to make the best decision. You may have this information to hand or you may need to gather it from other sources. You then need to consider it, produce a number of options for action, and then decide on the best. This is the decision-making point where you decide whether or not to act.

Here, the best leaders will also decide on a plan and what delegation approach to use. This is covered later in the book. That plan is then implemented. You will see that the diagram has "feedback loops" that allow for reviews, both after the job and if you decide you can't proceed.

This diagram may at first seem impractical, but just apply it to the last task your team did – did you go through all the stages? Consider a task that went wrong – at which stage did the problem occur?

In this chapter, we will help you make sure each stage of the process runs smoothly.

Leadership process

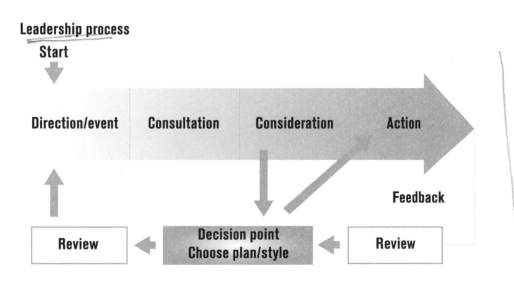

Start

Direction/event   Consultation   Consideration   Action

Feedback

Review   Decision point Choose plan/style   Review

Action Centred Leadership

Factors to apply

Having looked at the leadership process it is worth now looking at the factors you should consider when applying this process. The Action Centered Leadership model, devised by John Adair, provides a simple guide to the key areas you should remember when leading; getting the job done, keeping the team effective and supporting the individuals in the team.

If you neglect any of these key areas for more than a short time your team will not function effectively. For example, if you always concentrate on the job in hand but forget about maintaining the team and supporting individuals, the team will become unwilling or unable to do the job.

Task, team, individual

Try to apply this model, not just at the start of any task, but at all times during it. Good leaders will, during the "consideration" stage, also work out how they can best balance task, team and individual needs.

In other words, say to yourself, "this is the job we have to do, but while doing it, can I use it to build the team and develop individuals? Could I delegate parts of the job to provide development and challenge the team? Could I delegate it to more people to build team spirit?"

Keep thinking:
TASK, TEAM, INDIVIDUAL

Action centred leadership:
John Adair

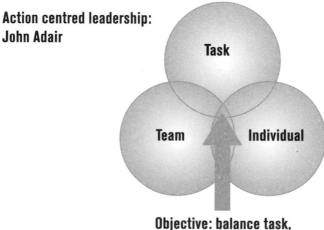

Objective: balance task,
team and individual needs

Critical leadership skills

Key skills

So far we have looked at the need to balance postive leadership input against negative forces, the process of leadership and the key areas you have to pay attention to when leading. The question you may be asking is, what skills do I need to be able to do all this? Over many years, research has been carried out to try to find what it is that allows an individual to become an effective leader. Pulling together ideas from many sources, the diagram below represents probably the clearest expression of the areas involved. Just remember it as: lead with "CARE".

Critical areas

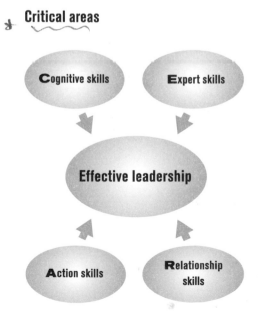

Imagine that each of the outer circles is a tree supporting your effective leadership in a hammock in the middle. This is the situation you should aim at achieving. But if one support is not present the whole hammock will be off balance. It may just hold together, but not work well. If two are absent then there is even more chance of it not working. So all these areas support the whole. The "trees" will be covered later in the book and suggestions made to help you improve your skills in each other area. Here is a brief summary:

- **C**ognitive skills: the ability to think clearly and analyse problems
- **A**ction skills: the ability to get things done, for example, how to delegate, motivate and communicate
- **R**elationship skills: critical leader behaviour and social skills, building trust and effective working relationships.
- **E**xpert skills: technical knowledge relating to your job.

Practice

You need to be as good as you can in all these areas to be able to become an effective leader. If you aren't perfect in any of these, don't worry, you can, with thought and practice, improve in any of these areas.

Critical leadership behaviours

The diagram on the previous page showed relationship skills. This consists of "critical leadership behaviours" that cements the relationship with your team and the wider social skills that enable you to work with others outside the team.

The "critical leadership behaviours" underpin the whole process of leadership. No matter how good you are at the technicalities of delegation, planning or other areas, unless you pay attention to these behaviours, you are very unlikely to become an effective leader.

They are more difficult to deal with than any of the other areas because they relate to who you are as a person and your views, attitudes and values. It is up to you to assess if you can live up to these expectations. They may seem daunting, but again, with thought, determination and practice, you will be able to achieve them.

Emotional intelligence

They are also related to the concept of "emotional intelligence," which links psychology to effective leadership. These are not abstact theories; they are backed up by hard evidence that shows the behaviours are the difference between the leader and non-leader, the team that will give superior performance because of their leader, and that which will not. They demand much from the leader but the rewards, both personal and professional, for you, and the team, are substantial. Below are these critical principles:

1. Self-confidence and self-awareness

This is the foundation of leadership behaviour, the ability to understand yourself, honestly recognizing your own strengths and weakness. It thus encompasses humility, (to recognize that you have weaknesses), confidence in your strengths, ability to admit your mistakes and an understanding of how you need to improve yourself.

It means that you also have to be consistent in your actions and attitudes; acting solely on your own feelings may lead you to be inconsistent or unfair. It thus includes self-control.

A word on self-confidence; you don't have to be an extrovert to be self-confident, or to lead. Abraham Lincoln led the United States through some of the most turbulent times in its history, yet he was quiet and introverted. He did, however, have confidence that what he was doing would succeed, and he managed to convey this to others. You can build confidence by gaining both experience and knowledge and then basing your actions on them.

"Don't waste enthusiasm"

2. Integrity

One of the most important things that a leader has to do is act with integrity. This includes honesty and underpins the trust between the leader and team members, allowing them to trust you. Without their trust you will be unable to lead any team.

Integrity means matching your words with deeds and honesty means being truthful and non-deceitful. Integrity sets out the rules by which you treat others and demonstrates your values. Think about the bosses you have most respected over your career – did they behave with integrity? In many surveys, individuals say the key behaviour they look for and admire in their leaders is integrity. It also means thinking carefully about what you do to make sure you are not swayed by impulses or temptations.

3. Enthusiasm and drive

Can you think of an effective leader who was not enthusiastic? It is enthusiasm that provides the foundation for the team's motivation. Can you imagine yourself being motivated by someone who obviously doesn't care whether a task is done or not? But it is also about why you want to get the job done. Effective leaders are motivated by a desire to achieve, that goes beyond status or money. The motivation is therefore internal, not activated by external factors such as money, position or personal power. Again, think about leaders you have known as well as your own motivations. Also, focus on how quickly you can identify people who only want power or money and your attitude to them.

Enthusiasm and drive also include determination and commitment. Leaders must be able and the ability to take a positive approach when things go wrong, showing that problems can be overcome.Good leaders put their energy into raising performance above the generally accepted level.

4. Empathy

Effective leaders have a genuine interest in the people they lead and understand them and their feelings. They want their team members to develop both as staff and as people. They know how to respond to different individuals and how to get the best from each of them. Good leaders show warmth towards their team, are approachable and go out of their way to support those they lead, whether taking time to talk to individuals when possible – "walking the talk" – or asking if they need help.

"Managers do things right, leaders do the right thing."
Thomas Cronin, management writer

Critical leadership behaviours

To get the team to show an interest in what you want to achieve you have to show an interest in what they want to achieve, too. This applies to everyone, from the most experienced member to the beginner.

5. Social skills

An effective leader has the ability to quickly build relationships, by establishing rapport, not only with the team, but to everyone he or she comes into contact with. Creating this rapport is based on the ability to show a genuine interest in other people and to try to find a common approach or mutual ground to enable something to be achieved.

In many cases, leaders need to build networks in order to enable things to happen more easily. The ability to find commonality and build on it is important in managing working relationships, dealing with conflict, and finding solutions to both long- and short-term problems.

Other areas

There are two other areas which are not part of the relationship skills or critical leader behaviours but are in the diagram on page 23. These are very important in making you an effective leader. Do not neglect these areas:

Expert skills

Linked to "expert power", although not a specific way of behaving, to be a leader you need to know your job. In other words you must have the knowledge and experience to deal with situations that you are likely to face with your team. You need not know as much as your whole team – you just need to enable them to use their knowledge and experience to the best effect. You are the architect, not the all-knowing hero.

Cognitive skills

Leader's have the ability to think clearly about problems, to form plans, make decisions and resolve other issues. They take a logical approach to tasks, but do not rule out innovation and new ideas. In this way, the best outcome can be found.

You don't have to be a genius, just approach things in the right way, and this skill can be developed.

Your own experience

Do these leadership behaviours link into your own experience? You will recall you listed the things that your best boss did that made them a good boss. Now list their leadership behaviours and tick off the ones that they demonstrated. You will probably find that anyone who you have trusted and worked hard for will have demonstrated most, if not all, of these leadership behaviours. Behaving in a way that demonstrates these principles will not automatically make you a leader – you need leadership skills as well. You must use both.

In the final analysis, the most basic principle to remember is "treat others as you would wish to be treated". If you follow this golden rule you will be using the majority of the key principles outlined above. You should think carefully about this; if you are not able to abide by the principles of leadership behaviour then maybe you should rethink your reasons behind your desire to be a leader.

Why your example is so important

The principles all come together not only in the way the team reacts to you, but also in the way they act as well. They will respond to your actions, and you are responsible for determining how the relationship develops – well or badly. It is important that you set a clear and positive example to your team using the principles outlined above. It sends out important messages that may influence team values.

Values may sound old-fashioned, but team members do copy the behaviour of the leader, as it is felt that whatever the leader does must be acceptable. Much of this happens unconsciously. You need to behave in the way you want team members to behave. The old military phrase, "lead by example", is a good summary.

The importance of example and its effect has been recorded throughout history. In the 16th century, Francis Bacon said, "A man that gives good advice and good example builds with both hands, but a man that gives good advice but bad example builds with one and tears down with the other". Whether you like it or not, you will set an example to your team. The only question is whether it is a good or bad one. Don't forget, in leadership, actions speak much louder than words.

The responsibility of power

Finally, if you have been given the power of leadership you must also accept the responsibility that goes with it. You should always remember that you have a duty to do the best for your team, both personally and professionally to enable them to do their best for you. "Serve to lead" sums it up well. To lead effectively, you must, by your actions, enable and encourage the team to do their best.

> **"Example is not the main thing in influencing others, it's the only thing."**
> **Albert Schweitzer, French philosopher**

First steps

Self-management and planning skills

Before you can start to lead others, you need to be able to lead yourself and be confident that all the preparation you do prior to a task is going to lay a strong foundation. For example, you need to determine how much time the job will take; how often have you found that a job ends up being finished late?

Although this book is not about time management, to be an effective leader you need to be able to manage your own time before you manage other people's time.

Prioritization, planning and problem solving are all part of effective time management. Only when you are able to do these things effectively for yourself can you then understand how to get the team to do them effectively.

Time management and prioritization

No matter how powerful a leader is, he or she only has the same number of hours in a day as you. It is what you do with this limited resource that determines what you achieve, both in your personal life, as well as your professional life.

Here are some of the key ways to make better use of the limited and valuable resource of time:

1. List the tasks you have to do each day. If you don't do them carry them over to the next day.
2. Prioritize on the basis of what tasks contribute most to "why you are here", the job that the organization needs you to do. Remember that these are primarily jobs that only you can do. If someone else can do them, delegate!
3. Within prioritization, sub-divide between what is urgent or non-urgent, and important or not important. Urgent and important is priority 1, urgent and not important or important but non-urgent, priority 2, and non-urgent and not important, priority 3. Reconsider prioritizations regularly. Non-urgent tasks will quickly become urgent!
4. Always delegate as much as you can, bearing in mind the skills and experience of your team.
5. Learn to say "no" to taking on work you don't have time to do.
6. Always set yourself and the team "SMART" goals – specific, measurable, agreed, realistic and timed. This is covered in more detail later.
7. Avoid procrastination – get on with it!
8. Put time in your diary to do specific tasks as well as appointments, for example, two hours to finish project x, one hour for telephone calls or an hour for planning next week.
9. Tackle large tasks in small stages and reward yourself, or the team, for completing each.
10. Prioritize telephone calls, and keep them short and to the point.
11. Paperwork: either deal with it, delegate it, file it or bin it, but don't leave it sitting on your desk!

Problem solving and problem appreciation

One of the main challenges all leaders face each day is the continuous flow of problems that come up. How many times have you unexpectedly been faced with a problem that seems to have no acceptable or easy solution? Unfortunately, this is the nature of the world and there is a limitless supply of problems.

However, if you can approach them in a logical fashion, the solutions reveal themselves more easily and the chances of picking the best solution increases dramatically. Tasks you may be given need to be treated in the same way as problems because you need to find the best way of tackling them. So in practical terms, you should try to run though the process below with everything you do.

This may seem time consuming, but with practice, and when dealing with smaller tasks, you will be able to use this process in a matter of minutes.

Jumping to conclusions

In many cases, we tend to jump to conclusions about how to solve problems without thinking logically. This approach often causes more problems. A good example is that we often automatically tackle a problem in the same way we did the last time it came up. Also, we may not actually identify the problem, but only a symptom. For example, "we need a new computer", or, "we need more filing space". These are not actually problems, but possible solutions to some, as yet, unidentified problem.

So let's approach solving a problem in a logical way:

1. **Identify the real problem**
2. **Analyse it**
3. **Collect information if required**
4. **Produce a set of options**
5. **Evaluate them and decide on the best**

1 IDENTIFY THE REAL PROBLEM. There are many complex ways to do this but for general day-to-day problems just use the "why" question three or four times. For example,
"We need to improve communication in the team." "*Why?*"
"Because there have been misunderstandings." "*Why?*"
"Because my instructions have been misunderstood." "*Why?*"
"Because I did not make fully clear what I meant." "*Why?*"
"Because my communication skills were lacking."

Problem solving and problem appreciation

At this point you should have produced an option that can now be turned, with planning, into an action plan.

2 ANALYSE THE PROBLEM. You now need to examine the problem to see how you can go about solving it, and to find an objective to aim for. Continuing with the example: Problem: poor communications skills on my part led to me not making clear what I wanted. Objective: to improve my communication skills.

3 COLLECT INFORMATION IF REQUIRED. You need to be sure that you get all the relevant information on the problem in hand then, within a reasonable time-scale. This information can come from any source, including asking the team for their ideas. They may be aware of things that you are not, or have knowledge or experience you don't have, so it is often worth checking with them.

4 PRODUCE A SET OF OPTIONS. From this information, draw up at least two or three possible ways to approach the problem. Don't just go for the obvious or "the way it's always been done before" option. Just because a problem has been solved a certain way in the past doesn't mean it is the best way to do it this time. Having a second option can also give you a reserve plan if things go wrong.

5 EVALUATE THE OPTIONS AND DECIDE ON THE BEST. Depending on the problem, evaluate the options to maximize benefit – bring in the most money, minimize the cost, maximize or minimize time – what ever measures you can use to show which option most effectively achieves your objective. Some tools, such as cost-benefit analysis, can be used for more complex problems, but for most, a simple list of "pros" and "cons" for each option, with some figures if possible, will be enough.

Planning

Planning is very important. It is often said that "failing to plan is really planning to fail". You now have your best option for solving the problem or doing the task, but before you can start work, you need to be clear on what needs to be done to achieve your objectives. Considerations here include: the steps or stages you have to go through; which order to do them in; and what resources are available, including time – a start time and a deadline. All this applies to your own tasks, as well as team work.

There is a simple formula that may help, from the famous poet, Rudyard Kipling. Try to memorize it – it is useful for many situations:

> "I keep six honest serving men
> They taught me all I knew,
> Their names are What and Why and When,
> And How and Where and Who."

If we use the example from the previous section on setting up a briefing process, this translates into action as:

QUESTION	EXAMPLE
What do I want to achieve?	Set up a briefing process
Why does it need to be done?	Misunderstandings have occurred, costing time and effort
When does it need to be done by?	The end of the month
How best can it be done?	By weekly team briefings
Where will it be done?	In the office on Friday afternoons
Who will take part?	The whole team, led by me

From this example you can then go into more detail in the "how best can it be done" section using the following guide:

■ Timings: what needs to be done when, especially start and finish
■ People: who needs to do what
■ Resources: financial, material
■ Authority: do you need clearance or authority.

Implementing your plan

Once you have assembled this chart you now have an action plan you can implement with your team.

If you look back at the diagram "the leadership process" on page 21, you will see that you have just run through the 'Direction/Event, Consultation, Consideration and Decision' process and are now about to 'Action' your plan.

Foundation skills: effective communication

The foundation skills of communication, delegation and motivation enable your plans to be put into practice. They underpin your key leadership function of achieving your objectives through your team, so you need to be competent at these before moving on to more advanced skills, such as creating vision and values and building team spirit.

If you can develop these foundation skills, it not only provides you with a base for the more advanced skills but allows your team and the individuals in it to improve their performance as well – because you will be communicating, delegating and motivating more effectively, they will be able to take on more work, be more motivated and

more effective. This will in itself make them more receptive to you when you use your advanced skills.

Basic principles of communication

It should be easy to get your message across, but unfortunately, bad communication is the cause of most problems at work. Evidence suggests that when we communicate, particularly verbally, only 50 percent of the message is understood the first time round! Understanding the principles of communication and how to apply them in practice will allow you to make sure that your communications are immediately understood. The simple model (below) demonstrates the process, and its stages.

Interpersonal communication   **Start**

You want to send a message

You construct your message

You match your message to the audience

You check their understanding and they respond

You send your message
(Distractions)

They understand your message

They interpret your message

They receive your message

So the whole communication process is summarized by:

You construct the message: the message you want to send is put together

You match the message: the message is constructed to suit, or match, the other person

You prepare the other person/people: you get their attention

You send the message: you initiate the delivery

They receive the message: do they understand it all, or only part of it? Are they even listening?

They interpret the message: do they interpret the words and phrases as you intended?

You confirm the message has been understood: you confirm this by using feedback, via listening and asking questions.

A simple message

The message is a simple one: for effective communication, the message received must be the same as the message sent. Just think of the number of times you have heard, "Oh, that's what you meant, I thought you wanted me to…" or, "No, that's not what I said, I said…" Understanding the model allows you to make sure that your message gets through and helps you avoid the pitfalls. If you can do this, you won't have to worry about the people you work with misunderstanding your communications.

In principle, communication should happen like this, but how do you make sure your message gets across? It's simple, by planning your communications – be they one-to-one meetings or team meetings. Here's a brief detail of each part of the communication process.

Constructing your message

This is the part of the process where you think about the message and structure it so that the other person will understand. Even in short conversations, you need to think about this.

The first part of the process is to put together the message you want to send to achieve your objective. So the first question is, "What do I want to achieve?" Is it getting a specific job done, briefing a group on the plans for next year, or talking over performance problems with a team member?

Apply these questions when constructing your message:
- What do I want to achieve?
- Why does it need to be done?
- When does it need to be done by?
- How is it best done?
- Where should it be done?
- Who should it be done by?

Foundation skills: effective communication

Matching the message

The second step in the preparation process is to fine-tune the message to match the audience. The audience in this case is obviously your own team, so you will need to vary your delivery to match the personalities of different team members.

The volume or detail you include also needs to match the individual. Compare how you would ask an experienced colleague to do a job, with an inexperienced trainee. The objective – getting the job done – is the same, but clearly you would need to include more information for the inexperienced trainee. Even with people of the same ability in your own team you know that some people will listen carefully and take on board everything you say, but others may have to be given the message twice before they can go and do the job. Give people as much information as they need.

Preparing the team or individual and getting your message across:

1. **Check they are ready to receive your message.** You should make sure that the time and place are appropriate for the delivery of the message. There may be other distractions in the office that cause barriers to communication, so double check that the team is relaxed and listening.
2. **Outline what you are going to say.** It is useful to give the receiver a brief outline of what you intend to cover in your message.
3. **Background.** Go over the background to what you're going to say.
4. **Say why it is important to you.** This is confirmation of your own assumptions and perceptions. It establishes why the message is coming and your thoughts or attitudes towards it. This tells the receiver why you are sending the message to them and conveys your interpretation. Make sure that they use YOUR interpretation when interpreting the message. If they don't, they won't fully understand what you want.
5. **Say why it is important and of benefit to them.** In any communication, the receiver must have some motivation to take the message on board. While this will be immediately important in some cases, you should try to do this all the time. Imagine telling a member of your team that he or she has to do a particular task. If you tell them how they will benefit – for example, by gaining new experience – this will improve their motivation to listen to the message and do the job.

Confirmation

Confirmation is your last chance to check your message has been understood. You must make sure that your message has been comprehended as you intended. This can be done through open questioning and active listening. Asking, "do you understand?" is not enough; the team or individual may answer "yes" just to keep you happy.

Open questioning

These are questions that do not have a "yes" or "no" answer. They start with "how", "why", "when", "where" and "what". A closed question might be; "Do you think this plan will work?" An open version of the same question might be; "What problems do you think might occur with this plan?" The latter will encourage much more information.

Active listening

When someone answers your question, listen to the whole of the answer – don't interrupt. If they have difficulty answering, help them with suggestions, but check the meaning with them first; "So is what you are trying to say is…" At the end, summarize and ask them if your summary is accurate.

Get the environment right

Make sure you match the time and place to the message you want to get across. Would you want to have your appraisal in an open plan office or in a private room? Fix a time in advance and ensure that you won't be disturbed. Also, always be on time. It doesn't matter if the person you are meeting is junior to you. Arriving late says, "I can't be bothered".

Communication principles summary

In practice, you should follow all the communication principles outlined above, and fine-tune them to suit your situation. Always use this basic structure to make sure your communication is effective:

1. Use a clear, simple message in a form that matches your audience.
2. Make sure the environment suits the message you are trying to deliver.
3. Get your audience's attention
4. Deliver the message in a way that enables your audience to clearly understand you.
5. Check the message has been understood by getting feedback through open questioning and active listening.

"Open a two-way channel of communication"

Foundation skills: effective delegation

It is very important to delegate tasks if possible and to match the level of freedom you give, "the delegation level" to the situation (the individual and the task) involved. This has the following benefits:

1. It makes sure the job is done by an individual or team capable of successfully completing it
2. It gives the leader more time to spend on leadership functions – for example, building the team, planning development and building working relationships
3. It gives the right degree of freedom to those doing the task so that they are not over-supervised or given a task they cannot complete with no support
4. It allows the individual or team to maximize their skills and knowledge development
5. It reduces sources of potential conflict within the team.

So try to delegate:
- Routine, minor and day-to-day jobs
- Jobs that other team members can do as well as you
- Jobs that team members can do better than you because of their specialist knowledge
- Jobs which will provide a challenge for those involved and help develop their skills.

THESE ARE OFTEN CALLED "LOW LEVERAGE" TASKS.

But try to do these type of tasks yourself:
- Jobs that require your personal attention as no-one else has the authority or experience to do them
- Jobs that involve the long-term development of the team – leadership roles. These include training, planning, gaining commitment, motivating the team, setting up control and evaluation systems, setting and agreeing objectives, crafting vision and team spirit.

THESE ARE OFTEN CALLED "HIGH LEVERAGE" TASKS.

Delegating high leverage tasks

As a rule of thumb you should try to spend 20 percent of your time on low leverage tasks and 80 percent on high leverage ones.

There may be exceptions where you need to delegate some high leverage tasks, for example, to develop the skills of your deputy to cover for you if you are away or if you are leaving.

Assess existing workloads

Before you delegate to anyone, first ask if they have time to take on extra work. Asking them is not enough – some people will take on work they cannot manage because they are worried about saying "no" to their boss. So before you ask an individual or team to take on more work, roughly assess their workload yourself before asking. If it seems they may have the time then ask them to confirm this.

Who should you delegate to?

Once you know that some of your team have time to take on the new task, you need to select the best person to do the job and delegate it to them with the appropriate degree of freedom to act on their own initiative.

Think about how you delegate at present; would you give a task to someone with no previous experience of the job or someone with a lot of previous experience? The answer is clear – you would choose the person with the experience. The same applies to the motivation to complete the job; would you delegate to someone who is motivated to complete the job or someone who is not? Again, the answer is fairly obvious. You would choose the person who is committed to completing the job.

Key delegation criteria

This shows the two key criteria for delegation – those that you are already using – task knowledge/experience, and motivation/commitment.

These also determine how much time you have to spend on supervision; inexperienced or unmotivated team members will need more help.

The lesson for all leaders is the more motivated and knowledgeable the team, the more you can delegate and the more time you have to concentrate on tasks only you can do.

In practice

In practice, there is a formula to help you. It classifies individuals for each job by their level of knowledge/ experience and motivation/ commitment. This helps you determine the best delegation level to allow them to successfully complete a task whilst minimizing your supervision time:

■ The Beginner is new to the task but very motivated – low in knowledge/ experience, high in motivation
■ The Learner has some task knowledge, but is not an expert. He or she is motivated to complete the task
■ The Regular has good task knowledge and medium motivation
■ The Performer has full task knowledge and is fully motivated.

Foundation skills: effective delegation

Classify team members

Think about those who work for you; write down one job that could be delegated to several individuals on your team. Consider, for that job, which classification each one comes under. Are they a beginner, a learner, a regular or a performer?

Also, think about one individual who does a number of different jobs. What classification does he or she come under for all the different jobs? He or she may be a performer for some tasks, but a beginner in others. This emphasizes the need for you to assess which category the person or team is in for each job you want to delegate.

As well as helping you categorize team members into the different classifications for each job they do, it also helps you see where individuals need to develop their skills.

This will be explored in greater detail later in the book.

How much supervision should you use?

So how do you determine how much supervision each individual needs for a particular job? Or, in other words, what is the level of freedom and responsibility they can safely take on without making costly mistakes? There are four levels of supervision, (below, left).

Do you ask them what support they need?

While you may have assessed the level of delegation the individual or team can take on, you may not have a fully accurate picture. Ask them if they can take on the job and what level of supervision they think they need.

This gives them the opportunity to take on more if they are happy or ask for more support if they are not. In both cases it allows you to maximize the chance of completing the task and minimizes the chance of it going wrong. Simply asking them will also make them feel more motivated.

Remember, you can still retain control if you wish in case you feel that they are overestimating their own ability.

CONTROLLER: You closely supervise the person or team, taking them through the task stage by stage, showing or telling them what to do.

COACH: You let them complete the task using their own knowledge, but you proactivley give advice and encouragement if you think it is needed.

CONSULTANT: The consultant is like the coach, but the advice and support is reactive – you only give it if they ask for it.

CO-ORDINATOR: The co-ordinator gives fully responsibility to the team or individual, and only co-ordinates the different tasks going on within the team. A reporting system is agreed so that you are kept informed of progress and completion.

How does time effect delegation level?

Think of a new skill you have recently learnt. You know that by using that skill, you can go from being a beginner to being a performer on certain tasks in only a few months.

The same applies to other members of your team, so you need to reconsider the delegation level you use for the jobs they do on a regular basis. In practice, if you are asking the same person to do a job they've been doing regularly and successfully for the past six months, you will be able to adopt a more "hands off" approach.

It is also useful to consider talking to each person about the delegation level they need for all their main jobs every six months, and agreeing it for the next six months. You should definitely try to do this at annual appraisals at the very least.

Can people go backwards?

For individuals to go backwards they need to have a reduction in either their knowledge/experience of the task, or their motivation/commitment. In most cases, people don't forget what they have learnt, so the chances of a reduction in task knowledge is small.

There may be occasional situations, for example, having not done the job for some time, or new technology or systems being introduced, that can result in a backwards step.

However, these moves occur much more often as a result of a fall in motivation or commitment. This may be as a result of boredom, problems at home, stress or other negative influences. The best response is two-fold: try to find the cause of the problem and deal with it, and give extra support during this phase.

Should I encourage people to take on more freedom?

In the time management section it was suggested that the more you delegate to your team the better it becomes. It improves their skills, motivates them, gets the job done and leaves you to concentrate on the jobs that you need to do yourself.

Agreeing to give more freedom to people, for example, by using the consultant level rather than a coach level, may be useful if you have an individual who you want to develop and give a challenge to. This is perfectly safe as you are still on hand if they need help. Better to give people more challenges than let them get bored, fail to develop and assume you don't respect their abilities or talents.

Foundation skills: effective motivation

In getting the job done, both effective delegation and communication are critical skills and will help motivate the team or individual. But it also applies in reverse; if your team are motivated then delegating and communicating will be easier – they will listen to you and be prepared to do what you ask.

Abraham Maslow, Hierachy of Needs (1964)

Self-growth

Public Esteem: achievement

Social: love and contact

Security: safety and shelter

Physical: food and water

We have also looked at how motivation is a critical component in assessing which delegation style to use. As a general rule, the more motivated people are, the less time you have to spend supervising them to ensure that the job is being done.

Different factors

One thing to remember is that different people are motivated by different things. As a quick exercise write down the following in the order that they motivate you to do your job: cash, holidays, responsibility, public achievement, contributing to the team and organization, helping others, personal development, clear objectives, support from your boss.

You may like to try this as an experiment with other people. Most people think that cash and holidays come at the top of the list but research shows this is not the case.

Maslow model

There are some simple principles that may help you understand motivation better. Abraham Maslow, one of the leading experts on the subject, said that we all do things for a reason, this reason being our desire to satisfy certain needs. This was put forward in his "Hierarchy of Needs", opposite.

Satisfying needs

Some of the things we want – the needs we wish to satisfy – are basic, some more intellectual. He suggested that we all have need for:

- Food and water *(physical need)*
- Safety and shelter *(security need)*
- Love, contact and group membership *(social need)*
- Achievement, status and recognition *(esteem need)*
- Personal development, growth and inner achievement *(self-growth need)*.

We are prepared to put in effort (work) to satisfy these needs. These needs motivate us to make sure we have food and water, work for promotion, try to achieve self-development, and so on.

These are shown in a pyramid format, as we move from the lower needs to the higher ones as the lower needs are satisfied.

Social needs

Assuming that most of your team have access to food and water, and have safety and shelter, this leaves the top three needs. Social contact suggests the importance of building team spirit. Think of examples where you have worked in a team with little team spirit, and one where there was a strong sense of this – in which did you work better?

Public esteem

The public esteem need can be used by leaders at work. Most people want to achieve recognition from their peers or boss in some way, either through rewards or promotion for jobs well done, or through a boost to their confidence and self-respect.

Exactly what form this takes varies with individuals: some will relish praise given in front of the whole team, and others will cringe at this, but be grateful for it to be delivered face to face with you alone.

Some may want visible promotion, others wish to be the acknowledged team expert, but don't want promotion. The public esteem motivator is probably the one that you can use most often, but you must know your team to use it effectively and fairly.

Self-growth

The self-growth need is perhaps the most difficult to quantify as it goes right to the heart of what people really want, such as personal development and the achievement of their own inner goals.

This can be the most powerful motivator, if you know what the individual really wants to achieve in their lives. It may not all relate to work, often involving family and matters

Foundation skills: effective motivation

"We do not only go to work to earn an income, but to find meaning in our lives. What we do is a large part of what we are."
Alan Ryan, management writer

outside work, such as climbing Everest or sailing the Atlantic. But helping them towards these goals via some part of their work will motivate them.

The public esteem need and the self-growth need can be used more than once – once promoted, you want further promotion and the same applies to self-growth needs.

Thus, by giving your team the opportunity to satisfy their own needs, you enable them to effectively motivate themselves at work.

Know your team

As was mentioned before, this view of motivation may contrast with what many people say motivates them. They say "money" as an immediate response because in some way they feel uneasy about admitting to the real factors.

This means that it is quite difficult to pin down what motivates different people. The only way that you can find this out is to get to know your team well and, if unsure, ask them! You should also never assume that the things that motivate you are the same as those that motivate others – but use Maslow as a general guide.

Changes over time

Also, be aware that motivators can change over time as individuals' priorities change. Marriage, illness, the arrival of children, and personal problems can all rapidly change individuals' motivators.

But what role do you play in motivation? Research has shown that half of our motivation comes from inside and half from external sources. To help you work out what your team want from their jobs just write a list of five key things you want from your job. Your list will probably be similar to most of your team, and include:

1. Having full control over work that has been delegated to me
2. Receiving recognition/praise for my achievements
3. Contributing to my team and organization
4. Giving me a sense of personal achievement
5. Allowing me to develop as an individual and professional
6. Providing a sense of challenge and responsibility in line with ability.

Here are a few tips to help you motivate your team:

1   Give people achievable but challenging targets which they are involved in setting with you.
2. Keep everyone informed about how they are doing on a day-to-day basis
3. Keep everyone informed about decisions, events or plans that may effect them
4. Delegate as much as you can so that everyone has responsibility and builds expertise
5. Allow individuals as much freedom as possible within their responsibilities. Let them decide methods, speed of work, stages within a framework where everyone knows who is responsible for defined targets, objectives or standards.
6. Establish a clear relationship between effort and reward
7. Encourage the team to become involved with planning, innovating and contributing ideas to improving team performance.
8. Make clear that individuals are responsible for their own task success or failure
9. Praise and recognize achievements when due.

Successful motivating

Ultimately, successful leaders motivate their team by understanding what motivates each individual and allowing them to motivate themselves as much as possible within an environment of on-going encouragement and support from the leader.

To do this you need to talk to your team and show genuine interest in them to encourage them to reveal their motivators. It is a partnership – as the whole leader–team relationship is – but it is your responsibility as the leader to make the first move to start the ball rolling.

Giving feedback

One of the main criticisms of all bosses is that they don't tell the people on their teams how they are doing often enough. It is very important to do this. Many bosses wait until the appraisal to tell people how they are progressing, but that may be months away. The answer is to give feedback after every important task, as part of being a leader. If the task is long, do it during the job. Your team needs your input.

There are two areas of giving feedback that need particular attention – giving praise and giving negative feedback. The first we tend not to do enough (when was the last time your boss praised you?), and the second is so often mishandled or avoided that it makes the situation worse!

Praise as a motivator

Praise is a good motivator and should be given when someone has made an extra effort, achieved something new or special, helped you out, or in some other way deserves it.

Just because they are being paid to come to work does not mean that everything they do is "just part of what they're paid for".

You know how satisfying it is being praised by a boss who you respect. It makes all the hard work worthwhile, so try to give it to your team when appropriate.

Structured praise

Whilst just saying "thank you" is a good start, you can give praise in a structured way that further motivates the individual or team. As well as saying "well done", also include the following in what you say:

■ What was good about what the team or individual did:
"You put in those extra three hours...
■ Why it was good:
...which enabled the job to be finished earlier than planned."
■ The impact on the team and organization:
"This meant that the other parts of the project could be finished early as well, which delighted the client."
■ What it says about them:
"This showed everyone how much you have developed and how committed you are to the team. Well done."

Try this the next time you give praise. It may seem awkward at first, but you soon get the hang of it. You can see how this format gives the person more valuable information than just "well done". But never forget that "well done" is much better than silence!

"Treat all members of the team equally"

Giving negative feedback

This is one of the most difficult and sensitive area you have to deal with as a team leader. If it is handled badly you can destroy the motivation and self-confidence of the person involved and ruin their relationship with you.

With the stakes so high, it is important to get it right. This does not mean avoiding it altogether, which just lets the problem continue and get worse. You can't make people accountable if they don't know that they are not doing what you want. The most important feature of good negative feedback is that it is designed to help the individual improve their performance in the future, not punish them for past errors.

Some guidelines

When giving negative feedback always use active listening and the other rules of communication, pages 32-36, to get your message across and make sure it has been understood. It is slightly different to getting a normal message over in that, if possible, you want the person to find their own problem and solution rather than having to tell them. If you realize your own problem you accept it more readily than if you are told! The best format to follow is:

■ **Find a quiet location where you will not be disturbed**

■ **Explain the general area that you wish to talk about** – "*you know that report I asked you to do last week?*"

■ **Explain why the area is important** – "*well you know that it has to go to the MD next week.*"

■ **See if you can get them to identify the problem you have in mind** – "*did you have any difficulties or problems that I could help you with?*"

■ **If they can't think of any, make a suggestion pointing to the area** – "*how about the problem analysis section?*"

■ **If they then confirm the problem area, ask them how you can help, share any relevant experience you may have had and with their agreement, work out a plan to deal with the problem in the future**

■ **If they still do not identify the problem then, starting with a positive note, describe factually what happened and look to the future** – "*well, although the report was generally good, you seemed to have difficulty in the development of different courses of action. I had a similar problem some years ago that I was able to solve, would it be of help if we discussed this?*"

This format is useful for getting your message across whilst not alienating team members by offering to solve problems for them. It also helps them to improve their skills. Don't delay in giving negative feedback – problems will just get worse.

Coaching the team

Most learning takes place through experience. The speed with which team members learn can, however, be greatly increased if the leader or a more experienced person guides the process, rather than leaving it to trial and error.

Training (generally knowledge, or skills, development conducted off the job) is effective, but not as effective as coaching. Coaching on the job is the best way to improve both performance, motivation and skills, not only for the individual, but for the team as a whole. It allows the individual to take on more responsibility, builds their confidence, sometimes enabling them to achieve things they never thought possible. It may also increase loyalty and reduce staff turnover. Coaching is a key skill.

Unfortunately, when coaching is suggested, many leaders say they have no time to do it – they have too much to do already.

So when do you coach?

If you think of the many ways in which either you or your staff find they need to develop their skills to enable the job, or new jobs, to be done, then the need for coaching can come up at almost any time. The team or individuals' opinion of you as a leader will be shaped by how you respond to this development need.

How do you coach?

You can't just tell people they're going to be coached. You need to ensure that they agree to the development and are thus committed to making it work.

To achieve these aims, you need to use some key skills on the way, which have been introduced earlier in the book: asking questions, make suggestions, giving feedback and active listening. Be careful how you make suggestions. It is much better if people can find their own solutions rather than use yours. Don't make suggestions until the individual you are coaching has run out of ideas first.

Preliminaries

Make sure that you won't be disturbed and that you are relaxed and supportive at all times during the session. You should spend about 80 percent of the time listening and only 20 percent talking! Prepare notes before the session under each heading below:

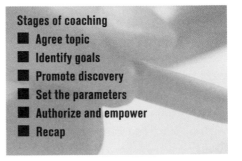

Stages of coaching
- ■ Agree topic
- ■ Identify goals
- ■ Promote discovery
- ■ Set the parameters
- ■ Authorize and empower
- ■ Recap

Agree the topic for coaching

This may happen naturally or you may need to discuss the areas in which the individual has the greatest need for coaching. Both appraisals and changes in skills requirements for the team often reveal coaching needs.

Identify goals

As with all goals, these should be SMART. Beware of over-generalized goals, for example, "To be better at using the word-processing package on the computer". This should be, "To be able to produce 75 per cent of documents successfully by myself using the word-processing package, by the end of the month." Beware of imposing your own goals. Try and let the team member find his or her own.

Promote discovery

This comes in three stages:
1. Active listening
2. Drawing out consequences from their suggestions: help them to think through their ideas
3. Sharing experience: show them that you are human and have had problems like theirs. Share solutions.

The objective is to help them discover the best way to approach the task themselves with the minimum input from you.

You should still provide a framework that includes details of:
- Resources available – personnel, finance and time
- Processes and systems that have been used in the past
- Past problems.

This will allow him or her to think of a set of possible options.

Set parameters

Now they have a set of options, you need to agree objectives, with guidelines on what needs to be reported back to you.

Authorize and empower

The individual will now have a set of tasks to perform. In some areas of coaching, for example, where the individual has to work outside the immediate team, he or she will need the backing of your authority, as well as the need for the co-operation of others outside the team. So you must give him or her clearance to do these things, and notify those involved.

Recap

To make sure you both remember what has been agreed, ask him or her to recap, particularly the action points. Remember that these are objectives and thus need SMART goals.

Running meetings

It is a fact that many team leaders spend a lot of their time in meetings of one sort or another. In many cases, you will not be running the meeting but when you are, it is very important that you get the maximum benefit from it; if you don't, you've wasted your time. Try to keep meetings to under an hour – otherwise people tend to get bored!

There are seven important aspects to making your meetings effective:

PURPOSE: why are we meeting?

PLANNING: plan and prepare what you want to happen at the meeting

AGENDA: put the agenda out well before the meeting

PEOPLE: don't just invite everyone automatically if they don't need to be there. There is no point wasting other people's time.

TIME: make sure you stick to start and finish times. Starting late with eight people waiting 10 minutes costs your organization a lot of time and money .

VENUE: often forgotten, but has a significant effect on how well a meeting goes. Is there enough seating, is the room too hot or too cold, is the table the right shape to encourage participation, do the aids work, are refreshments available?

MINUTES: make sure a secretary is appointed to take notes; you cannot chair effectively and take notes yourself!

Key action points for running meetings:

- Stick to start and finish times
- Make clear what the purpose of the meeting is
- Stick to the agenda
- On each issue, deal with facts, discuss interpretations, draw conclusions
- Be neutral and deal with conflict
- Ensure everyone one has their say; bring out the quiet people
- Listen to everyone
- Build a consensus during the meeting to gain support for proposals
- Provide an end of meeting summary
- Detail responsibilities for action; make sure everyone knows what they have to do.

Building trust and celebrating achievement

From a range of sources we have seen that building trust with the team is a vital part of being a good leader. But building trust is something that takes time and is done by actions, not words.

Building trust is linked to your values and the critical leader behaviours. The team should know you will be honest with them, treat them fairly, will be consistent and will support them – all the things that you want from your own boss.

Part of this is also telling them why they have to do various tasks and explaining why they need to be done in a specific way. This not only builds trust in you as a person but also builds trust in you as an expert because you know your job. This is your 'expert power'.

"Reserves of trust"

This is important as, on occasions – for example when time is short or there is some danger – you may not have time to explain why the job has to be done, and done the way you ask. It just needs to be done, and done quickly. You may not have time to consult as outlined in the leadership process diagram on page 21, so all you can do is make a decision and tell the team what to do.

But they will trust you if, in the past, you have built up a reserve of trust with them on the basis of your past explanations and consultations – referent power.

To build up this reserve of trust you need to give as many opportunities as possible to the team to input their own contribution on what they do and also allow them to participate in decision-making processes.

The trust you have shown them during these periods is returned on the occasions you have to just tell them what to do or ask them to put in extra effort.

Celebrate achievement

After you have reached your objective it is very important that you take some time to celebrate the achievement, and allow the team to do so.

Even if all you do is call the team together and thank them, that is better than nothing, but try to think of some form of reward – lunch at a local restaurant or a half day off.

This also applies to individuals. If they have personal achievements, congratulate them and, with their permission, inform the team.

This is particularly important for work-related achievements; gaining qualifications, doing a good job for another team are examples. Also, birthdays should never be overlooked.

"Inspire the idea of helping each other out"

Developing team spirit

In many organizations, teams don't work as teams but as collections of individuals. This is particularly true where reward is individually based. This reduces the potential maximum performance of the group as a whole.

Imagine a group of salesmen – some are experts and some are new to the job. If the experts do only their own work and never coach the new members, it will take much longer to get the new members performing well than if the opposite occurred. Building team spirit is critical to overall performance.

Mutual support

Whilst motivation is to some degree internal, for team spirit to flourish most of the effort must come from you. Building team spirit is critical to maintaining the team and allowing it to take on challenges and still succeed.

Your objective should be to build an environment where the team members will mutually support each other even without your input. This makes sure they are motivated even if you aren't there.

Have fun!

Don't forget the fun element. This is important for building enthusiasm. Make sure you encourage a sense of humour so that you and the team can laugh at yourselves and the problems you faced when you have succeeded. You know how much a small joke or funny story can lift the whole mood and inject another burst of enthusiasm when things may not be going well.

These are a few ideas for building team spirit:

- Train or work as a team as much as possible, e.g, team projects, meetings, training days
- Get the team to help each other – via sharing knowledge, experience and giving mutual support
- Make sure everyone has a "team" responsibility. The more experienced will probably be in charge of many work projects but it is easy to forget the newcomer who could be put in charge of a simple activity, which would give them confidence and a place in the team. An example is ensuring printing or stationery materials are in place
- Give the team as much information as you can.
- Always include eveyone in the team. Secretaries, support staff, temps and part-timers all contribute to the team, but are often left out. This is so bad in some organizations that these individuals become demotivated and the team performance suffers
- Where possible, institute team rewards – even if it is only taking them out for a drink at the end of a big project. Thank them as a team, as well as individuals.

Developing effective working relationships

The key "relationship skills" area of leadership competency can be divided into critical leader behaviours and social skills. Both are closely linked to "emotional intelligence". The critical leadership behaviours underpin working relationships with the team and the social skills with those outside it.

The skills involve establishing empathy with others, genuinely understanding their viewpoint and responding in a way that engenders trust. This response takes account not only of each individuals personal logical attitudes but also their emotions – which much of their responses are based on.

Experience

As experience and maturity build during your career you tend to become better at these skills – probably having found out that your chances of success increase if you take into account the feelings of those on your team rather than ignoring them.

Also, having a boss who was either very good or very bad at this will help you to understand them. Some people also naturally have a feel for how others are feeling or thinking. They have an advantage in this area, but those with less sensitivity can develop the skill.

Listen

No matter how good or bad you are in this area, one of the best ways to develop is to listen much more than you do now. Try to listen more than you talk, don't interrupt and let them finish everything they want to say. Then ask them why they feel as they do. You are then getting information you would not have got before, and are also letting them see your genuine interest.

Shadowing

Another very effective way to improve is to get someone whose judgement you trust and who understands this area to shadow you as you work – during meetings, speaking to team members, talking on the phone.

As you work they should note how you respond to others and how you could improve the way you do so. They will notice many things that you miss in the way your approach influences your working relationships.

For example, on many occasions, you may not give people the time to finish what they want to say, you may dismiss an idea without saying why. In the rush of day-to-day business you might miss this, but your shadow won't.

Two guides that might help are, "good leaders listen", and "always engage brain before opening mouth!"

"A leader is a person who has the ability to get people to do what they don't want to do and like it."
Harry S Truman, former US president

Advanced skills: vision and values

The advanced skills introduced in this section will enable you to understand how the more complex areas of leadership operate – building vision and values, developing team spirit, giving and getting feedback and coaching and relationship skills. These build on the foundation skills covered in the previous section.

Follow a plan

Vision is effectively, "where do we want to get to?" How you achieve it is, "how do we get there?"

Achieving the vision is just like following any other plan: use stages, delegation, objectives, motivation, feedback and communication.

Vision

Thinking about vision

In the rush of day-to-day activity it is easy to focus only on the short term. Having a vision gives the team a long term aim. This will motivate and inspire them over time, giving meaning to their day-to-day work. If the team has a vision, and believes in it, their performance will improve.

Think about this yourself: where is the team trying to get to and what should it be able to do in the future? What vision would inspire you? Jot down your ideas.

Creating a team vision

The vision for your team should be based on where your team needs to be, or what it needs to be able to do, to help the organization perform at its best in the future. If you have an organizational vision, use this to help build your team vision.

If the organizational vision is, "We will be the leading supplier of IT services by 2005", then your team vision could be, "We will provide the best Human Resources support to all departments by 2005". Your mission could be, "To provide leading edge HR services to the organization and thus improve personal and corporate performance so that we achieve our organizational vision by 2005."

If there is no organizational vision, you still need to make up your team vision. Go back to the question "where do we want (or need) to be?" In a perfect world, what would your ultimate team look like if you were leaders in your field? To help think about this, use the questions in the box on page 53.

It is often best to decide the vision and mission at a team meeting, as everyone will be more dedicated to achieving them if they are initially involved in creating them. Don't forget, this is a team vision, not just your vision.

Achieving the vision

To achieve the vision, and get to your destination, there needs to be some planning and objective setting. Achieving a vision is like a journey. As well as your destination, you need to know where you are starting from and how to get there. There are some questions in the box below that will help clarify where your team is now and plan how to get from your starting position to achieving the vision.

Team meeting

These questions are best discussed in a brainstorming session with your team. The rules for brainstorming are on page 61. Answers to the questions above should reveal the main actions you will have to take to reach the vision.

Each main area can then have its own specific SMART objective. In many cases, teams do not move from the vision to specific objectives, leaving them to try to achieve non-specific and non-measurable targets.

Values

It may be a surprise to see a section on values in a book on leadership, but it is critical to the way you lead and the way your team responds to you. What counts is how you view yourself and others, and how you behave.

Remember the section on critical leadership principles – how good leaders behave – and decide what your own values are in this area. Take a few minutes to write down your values and those you want to encourage in your team. For example, what role do integrity, honesty, supporting each other, producing excellent work, dealing fairly with everyone, helping people develop, loyalty, setting an example and team spirit play in your values?

If you remember, the section on "examples" said that the team will copy your example as team leader, so when you have thought about your values, talk to the team about them, and then abide by them. Remember, actions speak louder than words.

- What do we need to achieve?
- When do we need to achieve it by?
- What are our relationships like with: internal customers/ external customers/senior management. Do they need to be reassessed?
- What are the benefits of achieving the vision, both for us and the rest of the organization?
- Do we need new skillls?
- Do we need changes in systems/processes/physical assets (for example, IT, office equipment)?
- Where can we get feedback about how well we are doing?
- What do we already do that is helping us achieve our vision?
- What do we already do that hinders us in achieving it?

4

Leadership in practice
Problem solver: communication, delegation, motivation, advanced skills

Other pitfalls

Vision and values problems

Leadership in practice

This section contains all the practical information you need to do a task or respond to an event. It pulls together the previous elements to effectively help you use the ideas that have been introduced.

In addition, there are some extra ideas that will help during the leadership process. The General Process follows the structure of the "Leadership process" on page 21.

Vision to specific objectives

To enable your leadership to be effective, the team needs to know where they are going in the longer term (vision), general terms (mission), and what specific tasks have to be done to achieve these (objectives).

Each objective will be achieved through tasks that will require specific task objectives to be completed. At each stage – from vision down to specific objectives – everyone knows what they have to do and why they are committed to it. So the leadership process is being applied at general down to specific task levels – it's important not to forget the importance of the general vision level in the rush to complete day-to-day tasks.

Activation of leadership

The need for practical leadership is activated by an event, problem, or a direction from your superior. The first question you need to answer is, what do I need to do? If it is something you have been told to complete then what you have to do may be fairly clear, but if it is a problem that has come up, analyse the situation to make sure you find the real cause of the problem. See pages 29–30.

Information

The next stage is to make sure you get enough information to enable you to make the right decision. In the leadership process, this is the Consultation stage. As with other parts of the process, this is determined by time constraints. If time is very short, you may not have time to consult.

But whenever possible, you should maximize the consultation time you have with anyone who may be able to give you information about the task to help you make the optimum decision.

If you are short of ideas on the task then you can use brainstorming at this point to generate a number of ideas that can be considered in the next stage. Brainstorming is covered on page 61.

Consideration

Once you have all the possible information you might need, then you move to the Consideration part of the process. Here you consider the information you have, decide on a range of options, and then consider these in more detail to find the best.

Having now produced a range of options, your next problem is to decide which is the best. This can simply be achieved by listing "pros and cons" for each option. If required, you can also rate each pro or con on a 1–10 scale – some pros or cons will be more significant than others. For example, a con may be that the project will need a rearrangement of the office furniture, the pro that it will enable the team to do 50 percent more work.

This process should reveal which option is best. If costs are involved a cost/benefit analysis may help. For simple tasks or problems this process can be quickly conducted, possibly even in your head.

The issue of team involvement is also relevant. If you are asking the team to input their ideas, you may find that their input to the whole decision-making process is of value.

Decision-making

You now reach the decision point, where you decide if you can do the job, and how.

You may find at this point that you cannot actually do the task, because of a lack of resources or time, for example. You now need to return to the start of the process – the feedback loop – either to seek further information on the task or to tell your boss that the job can't be done within the parameters set.

Enabling

Having decided that you can do the task, you now need to produce a plan to enable it to happen.

Not only should you decide on the plan at this point, but two other critical decisions need to be made – the delegation level you will use with the team or individuals; and the way you can use this task to develop the skills of the team or individuals.

Your objective should be to get the task completed within the parameters laid down, whilst maximizing the freedom and development you give to the team and the individuals in it. Working out a plan is covered on page 31.

Leadership in practice

Setting objectives

To enable you to complete your plan you need to set objectives for those involved in the task.

You can't do a job if you don't know what you have to achieve by the end of it, so the setting of objectives, both for yourself and the team, is of great importance. You will have seen earlier in the book the SMART acronym. All objectives have to be:

SPECIFIC: what you have to achieve is clearly identified

MEASURABLE: you know when you have achieved it

AGREED: everyone agrees they can and will be able to do it

REALISTIC: the objective can be achieved within the resources present, including time and skills

TIMED: it is clear when the task must start and finish.

Challenges

Remember that to improve knowledge and skills you need to develop people through challenges – by giving them more responsibility at each stage of the task. This may take the form of doing the same task, but with you going from 'controller' to 'co-ordinator'.

After having decided on the objectives you now need to inform the team of what needs to be done in such a way that they all understand clearly what they have to do.

Briefing the team

One of the key things you have to do as leader is brief your team on the task, even if they have been involved in the development of the plan.

During this process you need to give those involved all the critical information they will need to do the job. If you leave out any of this information the job may not be done as you intended.

The following "BOGSAT" format will ensure that you don't miss anything out. BOGSAT stands for:

BACKGROUND: why the job is being done

OBJECTIVE: what has to be achieved

GENERAL OUTLINE: general description of how it will happen

SPECIFIC TASKS: detailed jobs for each person if required

ADMINISTRATION: reporting lines, supporting resources

TIMINGS: when do we start, finish, stages

ANY QUESTIONS: at the end, also ask if anyone has any questions – this is the last chance to make sure they all understand it before the tasks starts. If the team aren't clear, things will go wrong.

3 feedback

Monitoring

As the task progresses, your main function is to monitor how it is going and support the team through it. During this period you should give support as decided in your assessment of the delegation level for the individuals concerned. You may supervise as a controller for some and co-ordinator for others, depending on what they are doing.

You will also need to give feedback on how they are progressing. When doing this, follow the format on pages 48–49. This will make sure that the feedback is effective.

Getting feedback

As well as giving feedback to your team, it is very useful for you if you can get feedback on how the job is progressing from them. This benefits you in a number of ways – by giving you more information, as well as better quality information that can help you improve individual or team performance.

You can also use it to help you improve your own performance. The problem is that most people won't offer feedback to their boss unless they are asked, or feel that their boss genuinely wants their input.

Encourage feedback

You should encourage feedback as often as possible, both on a group and individual basis. Simple, open questions can provide a source of excellent feedback: "How best do you think we could approach this problem?"; "What are your views on how we could improve team performance?"; "Is there anything I could do as team leader to enable you to work more effectively?"

Once the task has been successfully completed you can hold an end of task "review". This is like a team briefing, but task specific. You should give general feedback on performance and then ask for feedback. The object of this is to allow the task to be done even better next time. It is not unusual for someone on the team to have spotted something that you may not be aware of, so this is a very important part of the process. This is the feedback loop that appears on the diagram, from action back to the decision point.

Problem solver: some basics

There are a number of problems or questions that regularly come up in the different areas of leadership we have covered.

These problems become fewer in number as you become more experienced. One main source of help is therefore more experienced people. Don't automatically assume they are always right, but assess their suggestions in light of other solutions.

How much participation?

You should always try to maximize the participation and degree of consultation with the team. This is not the same as letting the team decide what happens, although you can do this if appropriate and you delegate this to them.

Consultation and participation allows you to get information from them about their experience, knowledge, ideas and views that can help you make the right decision.

If time is short

In principle, you should still try to maximize the level of participation from your team. The secret is to maximize participation within the time you have.

As with delegation, the consultation and participation must match the demands of the situation.

This also relates to the experience of the team. The more experienced or knowledgeable they are, the greater the possibility that they may have information of use to you.

We don't have time to take on more work!

Almost all of us will have taken on work that we can't really do in the time we have. As you know, it becomes worse as time goes on and the deadline gets closer. To prevent this you must tell your boss the truth, and tell your team the same applies if you ask them to do more than they can cope with.

You have to be honest: "I can't take this on at present unless we delay something else". Make sure you assess the time it will take before agreeing to take on a task; and as a safety margin add on 25 percent to your estimate.

How can I stop mistakes?

Unfortunately you cannot stop mistakes, and should not try to stop all mistakes. Mistakes are a natural part of the learning process. You will minimize these by using SMART objectives and the correct delegation level.

Also if you encourage them to report back if they are unsure, this will help. If possible, allow the team to make learning mistakes in a safe situation.

VIDEO ARTS

"Projects work better if the people taking part have been involved in the decisions"

Problem solver: communication

People seem to take what I say the wrong way

This is a problem everyone encounters at some point. It is a result of some barrier blocking the communication you tried to get across.

This could be for a number of reasons – you don't include all the information the other person needs, or he or she didn't understand your perceptions of the subject, such as the importance of the task.

The key action that can avoid this is to have a confirmation session at the end of the communication process.

If there is any confusion about what you said then use the section on communication (page 32–36) to make sure that the message does get through. If you think that the person being communicated with did understand, but ignored the message, discuss this with them to find out why. You might like to send written confirmation of what you want in future to give you a record.

People don't seem to say what they really mean!

In many organizations, politics and personal fears mean people often don't actually say what they want to say. This is because they are worried about what will happen if they do.

For your team to be effective you need to change this, so people genuinely say what they mean.

If you encourage open communication in your team by being open yourself, then you are more likely to get the team to say what they really think. This does not mean that everyone will communicate in the same way – individuals will still use their own styles – but at least you won't be concerned about hidden agendas.

If you do think that there are hidden messages under the main message, use the general discussion format – open questions and active listening – to try to find out what it is.

There isn't a team-briefing system in my organization

If there isn't a team-briefing system in your organization this does not mean that you cannot start one for your own team. Whatever the attitude of others to this you know that your team will be "an island of excellence in a sea of mediocrity", as one person who did this said. Full details of running a team briefing are on page 83.

Problem solver: delegation

Why you might feel worried about delegating

Though you might feel nervous about delegating, in the end there is no alternative – you cant do it all by yourself. If you use the formats in this book, you will minimize the chances of any problems and bring great benefits to yourself and your team. There are always a few simple jobs you could delegate at once with little risk – start with these.

I can do the job better than the team

Yes, maybe, but should you do it if there are team members who can do it? If it is not a job you have to do then you should delegate it, provided it can be done properly by the other person. If not, coach them so they can.

I'm not sure about who to delegate to

Use the formats introduced earlier – you can then delegate effectively.

Do they expect me to have all the answers?

The team does not expect you to know everything – they probably prefer that you don't, all-knowing heroes can be a bit wearing after a while and it reduces the value of their own skills. You are there to do your job as leader, not theirs as experts in their own areas.

Why don't some people want to be delegated to?

These issues require the underlying problems to be identified through discussion and a solution agreed with the individual.

■ **They don't want responsibility.** In most cases, there is often a problem behind this. However, if they genuinely don't want more responsibility, then you should not force it on them.

■ **They might fail.** Generally caused by a lack of confidence in their own ability – you need to make sure they have the skills required, to build their confidence.

■ **They lack confidence.** As with the previous point, enable them to build their confidence by supporting them.

■ **They think you should do it.** They need to accept that the team needs to share the load and everybody has to contribute.

■ **They disagree with what is being done.** You need to find out why, and seek some form of agreement that either removes the problem or at least enables them to take part.

■ **They don't think the rewards are sufficient.** You need to establish what rewards they think are fair. For a problem to arise there must be a problem - try to find it and solve it by agreement.

Always delegating to the most capable

Although tempting, this risks problems if the capable person is off ill! It also doesn't develop the overall skills resources of the team.

Consider each task to be delegated. Could you delegate it to a less experienced person to allow them to develop their skills? You could always get the more capable person to coach the person needing development!

Not delegating jobs you enjoy but which others could do

Many technical experts fall into this trap. You must let go of jobs that you enjoy but others could, and should, be doing. Also, it sends all the wrong messages to the team if you are keeping all the best jobs for yourself.

Delegating jobs you should do, but don't like

There is no excuse for this. You just need to break the jobs up into small stages and reward yourself when complete. In many cases you may not like these jobs because you don't really understand or feel happy doing them.

If you think you need development help on these tasks, organize it. The fact that the leader also does horrible jobs sends a good message to the team and shows you are prepared to help out.

Perfectionism and mistakes

This is a difficult balance to strike. You need to do as near a perfect job as you can, but your team need to develop their skills, which inevitably involves making mistakes. Where there are legal, safety, "sign off" or other critical requirements that demand a zero error level then you have to take care – but it doesn't mean you can't delegate.

In these situations, delegate part of the task but check the work with the team member concerned. This will not take long and reduces the chances of mistakes. So where there are perfection requirements, delegate as much as of the task as possible but include a reporting back aspect as required.

In many cases we often overestimate the need for perfection and restrict the opportunities for our teams to take on new challenges. You should try to avoid this. Mistakes happen, but in safe situations, they are a vital part of the learning process.

The best way to avoid problems is:
1. **Give the person the responsibility they can take – agree delegation level**
2. **Set SMART objectives**
3. **Agree reporting back**
4. **Provide support in line with delegation level.**

"To make no mistakes is not in the power of man; but from their errors and mistakes the wise and good learn wisdom for the future."
Plutarch, Greek biographer and philosopher

Problem solver: motivation

What do I do with the demotivated individual?

Where there has been a fall in the performance, this is probably due to a drop in his or her motivation.

The key question you need to answer is, "why?" Here the importance of your ability to build trust comes in. You need to talk through the performance change with the individual and find the reason for it. Sometimes people assume that individuals don't perform well "because they are a waste of space", making no attempt to find out why.

This is a sign of a poor leader. In general, all the evidence shows that people wish to perform at their best, and if they are not doing so there is a reason for it, and the reason is a problem that is somehow restricting their performance.

Writing people off is an abdication of responsibility by the leader. This is because, in the majority of cases, poor performance is actually caused by a factor over which the leader has influence and control.

In some cases, the factors may be outside the team, such as a lack of resources, over which you have little control. Once you know the problem, do your best to solve it. If you can't, then try to work around it. This is all part of the leaders task.

What do I do with the demotivated team?

The demotivated team is much like a demotivated individual – you need to find the real problem quickly. Have a quiet word with team members whose opinion you value. If this reaveals the problem, then you can plan to solve it.

Next, hold a team meeting to discuss the issue and then discuss your plan for solving the problem. Agree a team strategy and then implement it, holding another team meeting to discuss progress in the following week.

How can I motivate a team already under pressure?

The main problem for teams in this situation is that their effort is not being appreciated.

The key is information, support and acceptance of their effort. Tell them why there is extra pressure, make clear you realize the extra work they are putting in. Tell them you appreciate it, and make sure that the number of mundane tasks is kept to a minimum.

You need to set an example in such situations, by working the hours they do and demonstrating the values you expect through your own behaviour. You should also be prepared to explain why the extra work is being done – they need to know to understand.

Motivating a team that is often apart

In many areas, for example, sales, transport or construction, the team is often geographically spread out, either on a day-to-day or a long-term basis. This makes it difficult for you to motivate them if they aren't present.

Where possible, get the team together – even one hour a week is better than nothing. Also, take every opportunity you can to get to see the individuals, both in the office (when they come in), or out on the road.

On occasions, not everyone may be present, including yourself, and this meeting may not take place at the office. The meeting should still go ahead – this is particularly important to newer team members. Encourage them to contact each other and make sure you keep in touch as well. Where possible, organize events, at weekends or after work, if the team agrees. So even if you only meet for a drink one evening, it keeps up the contact.

Motivating during change

Whilst change is going on all the time as organizations develop, sudden, major changes can be a source of deep concern. If these concerns are not met, motivation can drop rapidly.

You should always be aware that major change programmes within organizations always meet initial opposition, but evidence suggests that of those involved, one third will accept the changes, one third can be persuaded to accept them, and one third won't like them. So don't expect everyone to welcome the changes, even in light of your efforts, but most will accept them.

The key concern that causes demotivation is, "what's going to happen to me?" It is important that you give the team as much information as you can. If there is no clear information to date, explain, this and undertake to tell them as soon as you have any.

Motivating agency staff or sub-contractors

If you have ever worked as any of the above you will probably know only too well the difficulty of being accepted as part of a team when you aren't technically part of the organization.

Many team leaders have never been in this position, so are unaware of this difficulty. However, the effect on the team can be substantial. Even though contractors may not be official staff, they are, in practical terms, part of your team and should be treated as such. This means that they should be included in all training and social events that your team attends.

Problem solver: advanced problems

Coaching

These are the common pitfalls that cause problems during coaching. If the coaching of members of your team does not seem to be going as well as you expected, it is probably as a result of what you are doing rather than what they are doing.

To find out what the problem is, sit down with them and using active listening and open questions, try to encourage them to explain where the problem is.

Before your discussion, run through the list below to see if you can spot the coaching session problems.

Do you have specific and realistic goals for your sessions?

Do you have agreed objectives and an agreed time for the session?

Do you use the coaching process and structure?

Do you listen and watch?

Do you avoid trying to impose your own ideas?

Do you end the session with specific, measurable and timed steps?

Have you developed mutual respect and trust?

Does the coaching take place in a calm and undisturbed environment?

Are the questions open and no judgemental in tone and content?

Do you refrain from offering "advice" unless it is asked for?

If you have a solution, do you give the individual the opportunity to decide when and if they want it?

Do you use paraphrazing and summarizing to make sure you have understood what has been said?

Do you take notes of key actions and insights during your sessions to make sure they are not lost?

Do you check at the end of your sessions that you both feel the session goals have been achieved?

Do you ask the individual what their action steps will be and if they are committed to them?

Do you offer further support if required?

Problems during a session

An indicator of this is an increasing period of silence from the person being coached or apparent confusion about what is going on. Stop the session briefly and try to find the problem.

Apologize to them if it was something you've done and, if required, ask how you can help them get the process running again.

You may find it useful to revisit this list on a regular basis to make sure that you aren't doing things you shouldn't. All of us are human and after a period of time we tend to slip into bad habits, so a quick reminder is very worthwhile!

Vision problems

A team without a vision never performs as well as a team with one. Creating a vision with the team and then working to achieve it is one of the most difficult tasks for a leader. It is a long-term activity rather than a simple day-to-day one. These are some of the problems relating to vision that most often come up:

- The team seems to be less dedicated to achieving the vision than before
- The vision doesn't inspire the team.

The most important factor is the commitment of everyone to the vision. If the vision is right and agreed then you must motivate and inspire the team to achieve it. Don't forget that, unlike task objectives, a vision is much less immediate and needs more effort because it is something the team should aspire to. It therefore needs inspiration to achieve it. The exercises on pages 87-88 can help make sure you create an effective team vision.

There is doubt that the vision can be achieved

If the team was involved then they should have created a vision they all felt was achievable. However, they may need to be shown that the vision is still realistic perhaps through a plan that you could put together to show it can be achieved. If the team was not involved in creating the vision, then this is probably the cause of the problem.

People say the vision has no relevance to their day-to-day tasks

If you've got the vision right it should link into everything the team do, and that connection should be clear. Try to remind them how they will benefit when they achieve the vision and how day-to-day work builds towards it. At team meetings discuss the vision and show the team how progress is being made. Then encourage them to confirm their desire to reach it.

Values problems

The majority of values problems stem from the imposition of a set of values on the team by the leader. Because the team has not agreed these, they may not adhere to them – they have no "ownership" of the values.

Any imposition by the leader is counterproductive, as in the vast majority of cases, the core values of the team and leader are likely to be the same. By asking the team to help decide team values you gain their support for values you approve of as well. This can be achieved by using the techniques in the exercises section on pages 87-88.

5

Improving your skills
Learning and development
Exercises

Brainstorming

Meeting organizational needs

Working with your boss

Improving your skills

Even if you think you can already lead your team you can always be better! The first step in the programme to improve your skills is to recognize areas in which you need to improve. You can call this the "how well do I lead?" list! You need to be honest to complete this successfully. As with the other exercises in this book, if you cheat, you are only cheating yourself!

Tick the "Good", "Satisfactory", or "Could be Better" box for each question.

Planning and prioritization

How are your skills at:	Good	Satisfactory	Could be better
1. Identifying the real problem not the sympton			
2. Making sure you are briefed by your boss			
3. Allocating time to specific tasks			
4. Having a daily 'to do' list			
5. Prioritizing different tasks			
6. Deciding on an objective			
7. Getting information for a number of options			
8. Deciding on the best option			
9. Producing an action plan			
10. Regularly reassessing priorities			

Communication

How are your skills at:	Good	Satisfactory	Could be better
1. Understanding the principles of communication			
2. Putting together your message			
3. Face-to-face communication with individuals			
4. Face-to-face communication with groups			
5. Giving feedback			
6. Briefing a team			
7. Running team meetings			
8. Communicating with your boss			
9. Active listening and questioning			
10. Discussing problems and getting agreement			

Delegation

How are your skills at:	Good	Satisfactory	Could be better
1. Working out the job to be done			
2. Working out which jobs to delegate			
3. Delegating jobs to the right people			
4. Identifying Beginners – Performers			
5. Determining objectives			
6. Telling people what they have to do – briefing			
7. Getting feedback on job progress			
8. Giving positive and negative feedback			
9. Organizing an end of job review process			
10. Using the different delegation levels			

Motivation and team spirit

How are your skills at:	Good	Satisfactory	Could be better
1. Understanding your own motivators			
2. Knowing the motivators of your team			
3. Spending time talking and listening to individuals			
4. Maximizing the responsibility you give team members			
5. Praising where due			
6. Keeping the team informed about things that may effect them			
7. Having team events – briefings, social events, training			
8. Working as much as a team as possible			
9. Ensuring sub-contractors are motivated			
10. Re-assessing motivation within the team			

Improving your skills

Coaching and development

How are your skills at:	Good	Satisfactory	Could be better
1. Understanding the principles of learning and development			
2. Identifying, with individuals, their development needs			
3. Planning coaching within the team			
4. Acting as a coach yourself			
5. Regualry assessing your own development needs			
6. Having a personal development plan			
7. Sticking to your PDP objectives			
8. Using appraisals to help identify development needs and plan actions			
9. Producing a analysis of team skills required for the future			
10. Planning how to develop the team to meet future needs			

Vision and values

How are your skills at:	Good	Satisfactory	Could be better
1. Creating a team vision with the team			
2. Supporting the organization's vision			
3. Ensuring the team clearly supports the vision			
4. Ensuring the team achieves the vision			
5. Discussing values with the team			
6. Agreeing team values			
7. Making sure values are reflected at work			
8. Encouraging the team to monitor its values			
9. Supporting the team if the team's values are being compromised from outside.			
10. Making sure the compnay knows our values			

Building relationships: critical behaviours and social skills

How are your skills at:	Good	Satisfactory	Could be better
1. Treating all team members equally, fairly and with respect			
2. Acting with integrity at all times			
3. Setting a good example to the team			
4. Understanding the other person's viewpoint			
5. Doing your best for the team at all times			
6. Acting professionally at all times			
7. Never letting personal opinion influence you			
8. Helping the team build effective relationships			
9. Building networks to establish contacts			
10. Always working for a "win/win" outcome			

Identifying development needs

Now go through the questions and take any where you responded "could be better" and list all these under a heading "Priority 1", then take those where you responded "satisfactory" and list under "Priority 2". The priority 1 list should now be fed into your personal development plan as the skills that need urgent attention. Building your development plan is in the next section.

Other development areas

You will recall the diagram on page 23 which showed all the areas that you need to be an effective leader. The questions in the previous pages have mainly addressed the Action and Relationship skills but don't forget the Expert and Cognitive areas. Some of these will have been touched on, but you may also find it useful to consider if you need development in these.

List the key technical requirements of your job. Beside each assess how good you are on the "good", "satisfactory" or "could be better" measure.

Now list the parts of your job that take in "cognitive skills" – anything that requires a conclusion to be drawn from a range of options. Again, beside each, assess yourself.

For both areas, list the actvities that you feel you need development in, (priority 1 areas), and add them to your other priority 1 list. Your list of priority 1 development needs now covers all the key areas of leadership.

Building a personal development plan

You have just assessed your abilities at the key skills and produced a list of those areas that need work as first and second priority.

You now need to plan how you are going to improve your skills in each of these areas. This is best achieved by a personal development plan. It will also help if you understand the way you learn and how you can get more information to help you plan your development from yourself and others.

Understanding how you learn

Throughout life, we learn by a combination of passed on knowledge and expereince. We are shown how to do something, practice it and are then able to do it. If there is no-one to show us, we will try different ways until we get it right, but the process is really the same, no matter what is being learned: experience – learning – review – next step. This process is summarized by the diagram below.

The learning circle

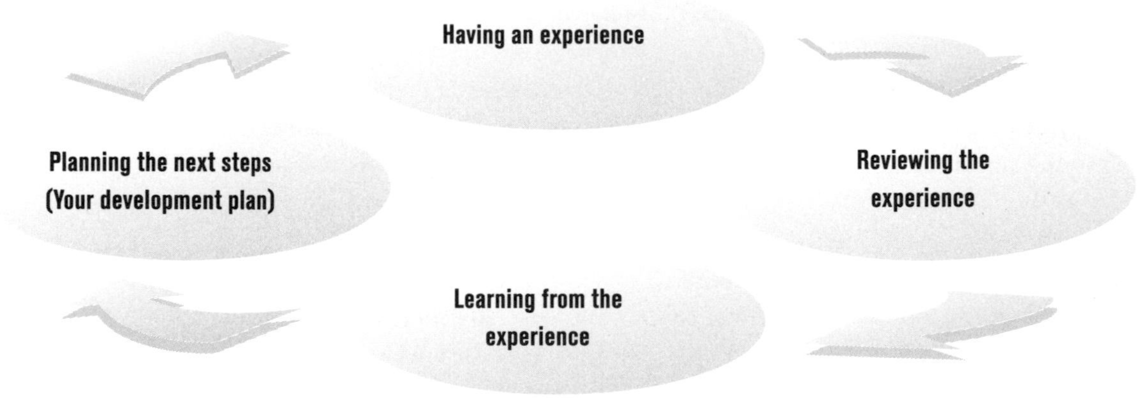

Having an experience

Planning the next steps
(Your development plan)

Reviewing the
experience

Learning from the
experience

This is the process you need to use reguarly to improve your skills: use your new skills (experience) – see how it goes (review) – learning lessons – planning how to do it better next time. This is not just a one-off; you should do this after any major task and review all your skills six monthly or annually.

The self-assessmment will have helped you find out some of the information on your abilities, but before embarking on your development plan you may need more help. The "Johari Window" (below) helps you to get and understand all the information you need to get better. It contains four areas of information on you, and you should think about each of these and how you could use them to help you.

Johari Window

	Information known to self	Information not known to self
Information known to others	1 PUBLIC KNOWLEDGE	3 OWN BLIND SPOT
Information not known to others	2 SECRET KNOWLEDGE	4 UNKNOWN AT PRESENT

Building a personal development plan

Information known to yourself and others

This is public knowledge about you, for example, how good you are at the technical aspects of your job. You know you can do it and you have shown your team you can. This is the easiest information to get.

Information not known to others

These are the things that you know about yourself but which others don't – your fears, feelings, ideas for the future, job preferences, who you trust.

Many of these link into the critical leader behaviours. They have a major effect on the way you act at work and you must consider them, to ensure that the positive attitudes are strengthened and the negatives ones avoided.

This area will reveal problems before they become obvious to others – better to address them now before other people notice them!

Information known only to others

We all have blind spots – doing things that we are unaware of but others notice. Have you ever watched yourself on video? Did you see yourself do something that you didn't know about but when you asked others, they said you always did it? This shows the importance of getting feedback.

You may be doing things that, unknown to you, are in some way restricting team or individual performance. A classic example is not delegating to people who could easily handle a task because you didn't ask if they could.

Here you can, if you wish, take a first step on your development road, by asking key members of your team whose judgement you particularly value for their views. The question to ask is simple: "Is there anything that I could do to help the team be more effective?" If you have the courage to ask this then you will be respected.

Many people, who have never done this, worry about possibles replies. You need not, as you will be given information that is of great value, that is, information you need to know, but at present, don't.

In many cases, the information gained this way has been of great help to team leaders and has enabled them to perfom better than before.

Information not known

This is the information about you that no-one knows yet. If you think back over your life you will have at various points discovered that you are either good or bad at doing certain tasks.

As we get older, more and more of these reveal themselves, but some do not because, although the signs are there, we never take time to look for them. For example, you may feel intimidated by certain people. As a result, you probably avoid them.

Giving presentations is a favourite! You may not like being in front doing the talking, but you probably never bothered to find the "unknown" reason why. Once you analyse these areas you discover the real feelings you have and the real problems. Once you recognize the problems, you can tackle them.

Preparation for the Personal Development Plan

Having assessed how you are doing in each area and listed those with the highest priority, you need to think about how you will address each. How can you turn each of these from a weakness to a strength?

To do this, you need an objective, based on the area, for example, "to make sure I brief the team on the task effectively". Then think about how this can be achieved, "using the formula in this book, write out briefing notes before each briefing", – and a deadline – "before my next briefing". You may also benefit from support from your manager or other parts of the organization. If they can help then you should include this in your plan.

On the next page, we start to assemble the plan from the notes you will have made.

**"There is no one who cannot vastly improve their powers of leadership by a little thought and practice."
Field Marshall Viscount Slim, British Commander, World War II**

Personal development plan

To build your overall development plan you need to produce an action plan to deal with each skill you need to improve. So for each skill under development priority 1, photocopy a development plan (opposite) and write in the name of the skill at the top. Then:

■ Write out exactly what the skill is that you need to improve. This may be "need to take more care in delegating to more experienced staff – tend to use the wrong style – too controlling."

■ Write out the steps you need to take to improve this in the "actions by you" section. This may include actions such as: fully assessing an appropriate delegation style before giving out jobs, attending a course, completing a team skills summary to see who can do what, holding meetings with team members to discuss their views on taking on more responsibilities or seeking a mentor. Each action you undertake should fit in with a specific area that needs improving. It may not just relate to time at work – you could benefit by reading a book on an appropriate area in your spare time as well.

■ Write in if your boss or organization could help you to improve in this area. This could involve discussing with your boss how they may have dealt in the past with problems similar to the ones that you now face.

■ Put in a "to be completed/achieved by" date. You must set yourself a deadline to have completed your actions by – and stick to it. If you don't, there is always something that needs doing instead and you will suddenly find that it is two years down the road, you've done nothing, and as a result someone else has been selected for that promotion you wanted.

Development Action Plan

Development needs

Development needs should include technical training, management competencies, and any skills you may need to develop for the future.

Actions by:

You	Your boss

Organizational support?

To be completed/achieved by

Improving your skills: basics

Time management

A major saving in time can normally be made via the use of delegation. A very effective exercise is the "What jobs could I delegate list".

Write down 10 jobs that you do each week down the left-hand side of a page. Then draw five columns to the right of these, the first column headed "name", the second headed "without training", the third headed "with training", the fourth, "training details" and the fifth, "time saving". Now consider each job.

Ask yourself if you can delegate that job to anyone on the team, either with or without training. If you can delegate, then write "yes" in the relevant column and the name of the individual in the name column. Then assess how much time you will save each week and put this saving in the last column. Once you have thought about all the jobs, add up the total time you will save.

In most cases leaders find that this process enables a 10–25 percent time-saving each week.

"What jobs could I delegate list"					
Job	**Name**	**Without training?**	**With training?**	**Training details**	**Time saving**
1. **Weekly sales figures**	Peter Smith	Yes			2.5
2. **Liaison with minor clients**	Ann Richards	No	Yes	Two weeks shadowing Andrew Thomas	1.5
3. **Sending out information to clients**	Bill Dobson	No	Yes	John B to teach him – about a week	(2.5 to John B)
Total					4.0 Me, 2.5 JB

Developing options: brainstorming

One effective way to find the different options for a task or consider a problem is to use "brainstorming". This can be done most effectively with the team or, if required, by yourself.

Brainstorming allows you to pull together all the possible ideas you have about a subject – it thus allows for new ideas and approaches, as well as those usually used. All the ideas can then be assessed and the best ones used.

A brainstorming session may only last 20–30 minutes, but it is effective because it removes some of the main barriers to creative thinking. For brainstorming to be effective there are five rules you should stick to:

"The way to get good ideas is to get lots of ideas and throw the bad ones away."
Linus Pauling,
American chemist

1. No criticism of any ideas until they are evaluated – not even astonished looks or giggles!
2. Encourage "freewheeling", where the group just bounces from one idea to the next. Don't slow the momentum in any way, just try to get the ideas to come thick and fast.
3. Get as many ideas as possible – it is possible to get up to 100 ideas in 20 minutes!
4. Write down every idea. This can either be done by someone appointed to do it, or individuals can write down their own ideas on a board. Some groups get people to write down their own ideas as they go along and then put all ideas into a central list at the end – whatever works best for you!
5. Let everyone think about the ideas for a few days. Many brainstorming sessions evaluate the ideas at once, but this means new ideas tend to be rejected. If everyone has a list of all the ideas for a few days the quality of the evaluation is much higher. Come back after this time and evaluate each idea – using pros and cons – then thin them down to about three good ones.

Work as individuals or in a group

Having understood the rules you can now run a brainstorming session. You can brainstorm as an individual or as a group, although if there's a problem it is probably better done in a group.

Get them together and explain the problem and ask for all the possible ideas they have, no matter how bizarre. Explain the rules, then off you go!

Mind mapping

You can also do this yourself through "mind mapping", where you put the problem in a circle in the centre of a piece of paper.

Like a tree, each idea branches off into another circle connected by a line. Subdivisions of these ideas then branch off further and so on until you have run out of ideas.

Improving your skills: communication

It doesn't matter if you don't accurately express yourself when you order the sandwiches for your lunch, but if you can't get your message across when communicating with your team or major clients then you are faced with a serious problem.

The event list (below) allows you to individually consider all major communication events and analyse your performance in each. It lists the main communication events that you may engage in on a regular basis and considers if you have room for improvement in these areas.

Set out the table as shown and put in each main communication activity you engage in together with the way you do it at present. To check you have assessed it correctly why not ask the person you communicated with what they think! This also encourages feedback.

This list will have given you an idea of the communication activities you presently undertake, but show how you could improve your effectiveness.

Communication event list

Event	1. Weekly sales figures	2. Giving feedback to team on performance
Individual who you have to communicate with	Peter Smith	All team members
Feedback?	No	Yes, but they say I am not always clear on what I want from them
Improvements or problems?	Tends to be rushed	Partial

Team briefings

Team briefings, as opposed to briefing a team, are a good means of passing on general information that may be of use to the team.

Team briefings are sessions, normally held weekly or fornightly, that enable you to tell the team any news, and allow them to tell you how things are going, about problems they may have and are a good time to discuss ideas and suggestions.

It is also a good source of building team spirit as the team is thinking together. Even if there is no team-briefing systems in your organization, it may benefit your team if you run these briefings yourself.

Use a formula

You need to arrange about half an hour to an hour for the briefing. Most people find that either Friday afternoon or Monday morning are the best times.

You need to structure what you are going to say before the briefing. The best way to deal with the part of the session where you brief the team on relevant issues is via a simple formula: progress and performance, policy and plans, people, points for action. Then you hand the briefing over to them for feedback.

So your notes should be written down under these headings:
- **Progress and performance:** tell the team how things are going
- **Policy and plans:** why things are being done in a certain way and what is planned for the future
- **Poeple:** changes in responsibilites and roles, not only in the team but anywhere it may affect them and the job you do.
- **Points for action:** what needs to be done by the team in the future, setting specific objectvies if required.

If there are certain matters that are bound to come up, then it may be worth preparing answers. If there are questions you can't answer then undertake to find out and let everyone know at the next meeting.

Practice

Now practice as if you were to have a team briefing tomorrow. Write in the information the team needs to be told under each heading.

The general rule should be that you should give them the information, unless there is a very good reason for not giving it. Remember that giving them information builds their trust in you and enables them to do the job because they know what's going on.

If you had a meeting today what issues would come up (write these down too). Do you need to address these now?

Improving your skills: delegation

The following exercises are designed to help improve your delegation skills using the ideas introduced earlier. To help you make sure you use the right delegation level for each of your team for the job, you should complete a "team delegation assessment".

Using the table below, write in the name of each team member together with four tasks that you regularly delegate to them. Indicate whether they have knowledge/experience of the task and whether they are motivated/committed to it.

Now write the delegation level you use with them currently in the "current style used" column; and in the "possible future style" column put the level that the formula suggests you should use,

	Task 1	Task 2	Task 3	Task 4
Team member's name	John Smith			
Tasks he/she does regularly	Weekly sales figures			
Knowledge/ experience?	Yes, high			
Motivated/ committed?	Yes, high			
Current style used	Consultant			
Possible future style?	Co-ordinator			
Style agreed ?	Co-ordinator			

bearing in mind the knowledge/ motivation assessment. Does this agree with the level you are currently using?

The last column is headed "style agreed". This will allow you to discuss your assessment for each task with the individual and ask for their views. You can then agree a style.

Challenge

Don't forget that where possible you should give team members a challenge, so try to be more "hands off" than "hands on". Also remember that with time, people develop, so ideally you

need to repeat this process three times a year for 15–30 minutes.

You will find that you will naturally tend to use one delegation level more often than others, which may lead to ineffective delegation. By using the formula you should get the level right, but first get the agreement of the individual concerned.

Each delegation level has advantages and disadvantages that you should bear in mind. The table below gives you a summary of the benefits, risks and examples of best use for each delegation level:

Style	Benefits	Risks	Example Situation
Controller	Rapid decisions if time is short, clear objectives and performance requirements.	No involvement from individual/team. Takes a lot of your time.	For team members with little experience, especially on critical jobs.
Coach	Builds confidence. Small risk of mistakes, but encourages them to take responsibility.	Can be time consuming and can leave individual dependent on you.	When people have some experience, but still need a fair amount of support.
Consultant	Builds commitment and encourages taking on of responsibility.	Decision-making process may take longer. Team can get asked too many questions.	For experienced staff, who can contribute ideas, and who can work without you at hand.
Co-ordinator	Gives you maximum time to do other tasks. Builds team innovation and motivation.	May end up with a group of individuals not a team.	For motivated and experienced staff who can solve most problems.

Improving your skills: motivation

To be able to help your team to be fully motivated you need to understand which individuals are motivated by which motivating factors. You will recall Maslow's "Hierarchy of Needs" – here are some of the main motivating factors from the workplace.

Write down a list of your team members' names, and next to each name add which of the following motivating factors you think applies to them:

Money: some form of financial reward
Status: public status of some sort
Responsibility: extra responsibility
Personal thanks: some form of personal thanks or gift from you
Public praise: some form of public praise that gets them noticed
Challenge: a new type of challenge they enjoy, for example, working with new people or new technology

Freedom: more freedom than they currently have. This may be linked to extra responsibility.

Key motivators

You will find that while all of these will probably be welcomed by most people, one or two of them will be wanted much more than the others. These are the key motivators for that person.

You don't have to work it all out for yourself. You can, with listening and open questions, often discover which of these motivators applies to which individual by talking to them about what they want out of their job.

Having thought about the motivators for your team here are some rewards that could be used for these individuals. Try these, or your own ideas, to see if they work.

MONEY. For some people extra money is better than other motivators, but these are the exceptions. Only about 10 percent of your workforce will want this.

PUBLIC PRAISE. A letter of thanks copied to your boss, a mention at a team briefing; anything that makes it clear that to others, possibly senior management, that they have done well.

PERSONAL THANKS. Just thanks from you as leader is effective for many people. For special effort, some kind of gift is a good idea.

STATUS. Promotion or some form of identifiable public status.

RESPONSIBILITY. More responsibility, even if it is a more hands-off delegation level by you, either at once or in the future works for some people.

CHALLENGE. Offering a challenging assignment or even just a more hands-off delegation level may be effective.

FREEDOM. Ability to do their work in the way they want or when they want.

Improving your skills: advanced

Creating a team vision

The team vision should inspire the team. It should say where the team wants to be in the future. Creating this vision should be done with everyone's participation; it needs to be something that all support. You can't just impose your own ideas. However, you need to plan the process, so think about how to get them coming up with ideas on the subject. Try to bring as much inspiration to the session as you can.

The first stage is to write down, "where do we, as a team, really want to be in the future?" In other words, if you could determine the future, how would you see the team in, say five years time? Ask the team to individually write down their own vision and then get them to divide into groups to discuss their ideas. After a few minutes, get each group to produce one idea and from this, distill a team vision that everyone can agree to. The vision should be a short statement of where the team is going.

Creating a team mission

The mission is different to the vision in that it says, "what are we here for? What is our purpose?" Run through the same process as you did with the team vision. You may find that to get to the real mission you have to cut through layers

of detail. To do this, when the team has come up with a mission, for example, "to supply best practice IT support", ask them, "why is this important?"

Ask the team to list the three most important things they have to do to enable them to achieve the mission; these indicate your key actions.

Thinking about values and critical behaviours

To help you develop a set of clear values and behaviours for you and the team, you need to list those values that people think are important. You can do this by asking a range of questions:

- ■ "List the core values that you bring to work."
- ■ "If you won £2 million on the lottery, which values would you still stick to?"
- ■ "What are the core values you hope your children think you have?"

Some common answers

Values: honesty, integrity, respect for others, fairness, trust, openness, professionalism.

Behaviours: professionalism, self-awareness, enthusiasm, ability to establish mutual respect, ability to establish common ground.

Improving your skills: advanced

Get a consensus

It may also be useful to agree what each value actually means to everyone because it has different meaning for different people.

Get the team to individually write down their own values and then ask them to select their top three by removing the ones they would be prepared to compromise on. Once everyone has done this, compile a team list, indicating the most popular choices.

The values can also be turned into behaviours – acting with integrity, showing respect for others, being fair, showing trust. In practice, it is essential that this happens. There is little point trying to impose your values on the team. They will almost definitely have the same core values as you anyway, so it makes sense to get the team to determine the team values. Imposing them will result in failure.

Having established the team values you need to get the team to list the behaviours, or actions, that they need to carry out to demonstrate these values. They should be encouraged to behave according to this list as individuals and motivate each other to stick to it. You should also stress the importance of the team monitoring their own, and other team members', adherence to the agreed values.

Make sure that team activities, rewards and policies support the values. Talking about values with the team is also beneficial. It encourages an open and honest discussion, which helps improve team culture.

Coaching

In the section on coaching there is a detailed structure for running a coaching session, in the problem section there are details of common pitfalls that are associated with this subject. Opposite is a detailed set of questions you should ask to help your coaching session along.

STEPS	QUESTIONS
Agree the topic	What is the topic you would like to discuss?
Identify the goals	What would a solution to this problem be?
	What would you like to gain from this session?
	Why do you think that would be beneficial for you?
	How long do you think we need to achieve this?
Promote discovery (where are we now?)	What is the present situation?
	What has been done already?
	What has happened as a result of that?
	What evidence is there of any problems?
	Has anyone else had this experience or problem?
	Where exactly is the problem?
	Who else is involved or responsible?
	How do they view the situation?
Promote discovery (what are the options?)	What options have you thought of?
	What would you do?
	What would be the first step?
	How have others tackled this type of task in the past?
	What other ideas or opinions do you have?
	What are the costs or benefits of the various options?
	Without asking for a decision, which option do you think is most viable?
Recap	What are the next steps?
	Which steps do you plan to take?
	When will you start the process?
	What problems or obstacles can you foresee?
	What support will you need from me or others?
	Who can you get to help you?
Giving feedback/ideas	I have some ideas/suggestions/feedback. Would you like to hear them?
	How do you feel we're progressing towards our goals?
	Is there anything else that you would like to do or think that we should cover?
	Do you feel we're going in the right direction?

Meeting organizational needs

These exercises will help you see if your team is meeting the needs of the organization – the "why are we here?" question. Write "why are we here?" on the top of a piece of paper and underneath, list all the jobs and services the team provides to the organization.

This can be used in two ways. Firstly, if you look down the list and summarize in one sentence what you do, you can use this as a good basis for formulating the team's vision (long-term statement of intent) and mission (shorter-term statement of what you need to deliver).

Assessing performance

Go down your list and assess the team performance in each of the entries, as good, satisfactory or poor.

If you are not sure, the best way to find out the real performance level is to ask those you work for.

This is also a very good way of finding out about things you could do to improve the way you provide your team services. This also improves your relationship with them.

The ratings you now have will show which areas require improvement and which are satisfactory. You should look in detail at why there are areas that need improvement. This could be because of short fallls in :

■ Material resources: not having enough computers, for example
■ Human resources: staff, training, knowledge, experience, motivation
■ Time: not being given enough time to complete the job with the resources you have
■ Financial resources: not having enough money to enable the job to be done well.

Identify which of these causes team performance to fall short of satisfactory (at the least), and look at ways of addressing lack of resources.

SWOT analysis

Having assessed how you are at meeting the needs of the organization you should also feed this into an analysis of where the team is now and what it may generally need to do in the future.

One way to do this is to do a SWOT analysis: Strengths, Weaknesses, Opportunities and Threats. On the top of a piece of paper write the objective of your team and underneath write the four headings. Under each, list the factors within the team that are strengths and those that are weaknesses. Under Opportunities and Threats write down the factors, both internal and external, that may affect the ability of the team to do the job.

Team skills and knowledge assessment

From this SWOT analysis you can now determine the general skills or knowledge shortages in your team. You need to identify how you are going to address them. Discuss how you will address the results of your analysis with the team. Preparing your own notes beforehand will help you in this.

Matching skills to tasks

To go from the general concepts of the SWOT to the more specific needs of team skills you have to compile a list of all the skills you need to have in the team to function effectively.

The easiest way to do this is to go back to the list of tasks the team does for the organization (see page 90) and work out what skills are required to do each of those jobs.

Some important questions you should ask are:

- What skills do the team need? Link this to the job the team has to do
- What skills do the team have? Break this down into individual skills. Do a rough note on each detailing any obvious shortfalls
- Do the skills we have match the skills we need? Compare the two and see if you need to improve the team's skills.

It is important that you do this because whilst all the people in your team may be well qualified in the areas they deal with, there may be another area in which the team has to work where no one has the relevant skills. The solution to this is either recruit a new person to cover this area (which can be expensive) or provide further training for some of the existing team.

Team development plan

So you should now have a list of skills shortfalls in the team. Go back to the personal development plan form on page 79 and use it as a basis for a team development plan. For each team skill requiring development write out a form detailing your plan to address the shortfall.

In this way you should be able to build up the skills within your team to make sure that you are able to fully meet client's or bosses' demands.

Working with your boss

At this point don't forget your own boss. Your relationship with him or her is critical. You need to "lead upwards" with your boss.

All those things that you find your team might do that worry or annoy you will also be things that, if you do them, will annoy or worry your boss, such as giving bad news at the last minute.

If your boss has more experience than you, you might also think about being coached by him or her, though this may take some encouragement.

You can set an example upwards by using the critical leader behaviours in your dealings with him or her.

Further development

In addition to the concepts put forward so far, there are other ideas that will help to improve your overall skills.

One of these is to try to broaden your knowledge of your organization, so that you understand how it works as a whole. The ability to take a corporate overview rather than a narrow functional view distinguishes the strategic leader from the rest.

One of the most effective forms of development you can undertake is via a mentor. This is a more experienced person, who is not on your direct reporting line, who provides general advice on improving skills and resolving problems, particularly those relating to relationships at work. As we saw earlier, these are key to effective leadership. Try to find a mentor, and also be a mentor for a less experienced person. You will learn just as much from being a mentor as being mentored!

Always focus on the people

Recently, some major international organizations have identified gaining extra performance through leadership excellence as the key element in future competitive advantage. The bottom line is important, but with exceptional performance through people it could be much higher. To summarize, the short leadership course works well:

The six most important words:
"I admit I made a mistake"
The five most important words:
"I am proud of you"
The four most important words:
"What do you think?"
The three most important words:
"Please would you"
The two most important words:
"Thank you"
The one most important word:
"We"
The least most important word:
"I".

Conclusion

Having read this book you will now understand much more about how to be an effective leader, but that won't make you one.

Much of what you have read is about structures and formats to help you get it right, but no matter how good you are at using these, if you forget that leadership is about people you won't succeed.

Relationships

Ultimately, leadership relies on a personal bond you build with your team, and while books can help with the mechanics, that bond can only be established by you in your own personal way.

Those who have contributed to the ideas in this book have been leaders in a whole range of areas, from commercial organizations, to disaster relief charities to those who have led and fought in battle. For all of them, it is the personal relationship with those they have led that enabled both them and their teams to achieve so much.

Even in the ultimate test of leadership on the battlefield it is the bond that the leader has with the team that enables everyone to face and overcome the dangers as team. Those have been through this trial know that it is not rank, status or fear that makes the team do as the leader asks, but their respect and trust for the leader as a person and his respect and trust in them.

Good luck in your quest to become a leader at whatever level or in whatever area you choose. Resolve to be a "leader for good" as well as a "good leader".

Lao Tzu

A fitting end are the words of Lao Tzu in the six century BC, showing that good leadership has really remained the same for the past 2,500 years:

A leader is best
when people rarely know he exists;
not so good when people serve and
acclaim him;
worst when they despise him,
Fail to honour people
they fail to honour you.
But of a good leader, who talks little,
when his work is done, his aim fulfilled,
They will all say, "We did this
ourselves."

Index

Further reading

Working with Emotional Intelligence, Daniel Goleman (Bloomsbury, 1998). A detailed look at the critical importance of the relationship skills needed for effective leadership. 400 pages.

Motivation and Leadership at Work, Steers, Porter and Bigley (McGraw Hill, 1996). A very comprehensive look at the theories of leadership and motivation in relation to their application at work. Good analysis some of the latest ideas and evidence. 750 pages.

Build a Great Team, Ros Jay (Institute of Management/Pitman, 1995). A look at some of the practical day-to-day aspects of running a team, the problems that often arise and suggestions on solving them. 170 pages.

Motivating People, Trevor Bentley (McGraw Hill, 1996). A good look at the principles and practice of developing learning, facilitation, coaching, feedback and other skills needed to help your team improve. 120 pages.